Takeoff

ALSO BY DANIELE DEL GIUDICE

Lines of Light

Daniele del Giudice

Takeoff

THE PILOT'S LORE

Translated from the Italian
by Joseph Farrell

Harcourt Brace & Company

NEW YORK   SAN DIEGO   LONDON

© Giulio Einaudi editore s.p.a., 1994
English translation © Joseph Farrell, 1996

This is a translation of STACCANDO L'OMBRA DA TERRA

Library of Congress Cataloging-in-Publication Data
Del Giudice, Daniele.
[Staccando l'ombra da terra. English]
Takeoff: the pilot's lore / Daniele del Giudice;
translated from the Italian by Joseph Farrell.
p.   cm.
0-15-100269-x
I. Flight—Fiction.   I. Farrell, Joseph.   II. Title.
PQ4864.E4377S7313   1997
853'.914—dc20   96-45987

ВТ 20.00 /10.68   8/97
Text set in Granjon
Designed by Lori McThomas Buley
Printed in the United States of America
First edition

A B C D E

Contents

Takeoff

All because of the Mistake

THERE IS NEITHER a precise moment nor an agreed day, no forewarning conveyed by any external sign, by any alteration in behavior or change in the surrounding landscape, no visible deviation from humdrum routine—the sun striking across the runway, the runway stretching towards the sea—nothing whatsoever to give any indication that, for you, that moment has arrived when, as in the blackest of nightmares, you find yourself in an airplane without passengers, without pilots, without any living being apart from yourself. There is no ban on talking aloud, no one will even notice if you sing or if you break into a sweat, you may turn to your right and stare at the place normally filled by your instructor, you may consider that emptiness the most painful of all representations of the absolute void or as the most poignant of all sensations of abandonment. You are, of course, at liberty to haul back the levers, switch off the propeller, open the doors, undo the safety belts, climb out waving your arms over your head, and leave it to someone else to come and move the plane you are abandoning where it stands, lined up at the beginning of the runway for your first solo takeoff. An immensely wise decision, perhaps even an honorable decision, but do you dare make such a decision? Your instructor is outside the hangar, looking on with no less perplexity, with no less concern than you are showing yourself; you are familiar with the mannerisms of flying instructors, with that way they have of gazing at the sky which makes them one with soothsayers, meteorologists and worried fathers: inside the airfield, all traffic has been suspended for your first solo takeoff; however early it may be and however deserted the surroundings seem, there is always a vast, unsuspected audience for anyone about to cut a pathetic figure.

So there you are, whatever instinct or pain or malformation of the unconscious may have led you to believe yourself capable of facing such a situation, there you are with your feet desperately jammed on the brakes to stop the plane making up its mind for you, and taxying down the runway by itself, presumably for its own first solo takeoff; at this point, turning back would be more complicated than carrying on, so, having made the most detailed arrangements to box yourself in, you can once more delude yourself that you have no choice, and that now, at the very last minute, tense and silent, your only wish is to see how it will all end, to go through with it, to make for the far point on the runway, for that moment of disequilibrium which, as you lift your shadow from the earth, accompanies the ascent and the climb into the skies.

A matter of moments ago, arms imperturbably

folded, a flying instructor had been seated at your side as your shield against all responsibility for error (the God Error) or accident; a matter of moments ago the day was unremarkable and unpredictable, and you ache to return to that moment, or even to the one preceding it, to the moment of heedless tranquillity on the apron as you carried out routine checks, moving round the aircraft as though it were freshly delivered from the factory and you were its first inspector, whereas you were no more than an apprentice pilot on a plane meticulously checked by mechanics that day, every day: you would gladly return to the time when you sat in the cockpit fingering the instruments, ticking off items from a checklist you knew by heart, following a daily liturgy, reciting prayers from a manual of "All OK," waiting for that very last moment when, as was his wont, your instructor, one of those people who never had time to dally, would finally clamber aboard and allow the engine to be started up. Bruno was not simply a captain, he was an Indian chief, an old-style Indian chief of few words and fewer explanations. Bruno was a teacher who disdained explanations, and how this was possible in matters of such delicacy will be explained later on. For Bruno, it was an article of faith that the concept of maneuver entailed absolute discipline and rigor, but his concern was with intuition; a correctly executed maneuver was less than nothing, scarcely the bare minimum, as he did not exactly say but certainly made you understand; flying was more than the nicely executed maneuver. He never explained, he behaved as though you were already aware and what you did not know, that is everything, you were left to pick up from the silence of his eyes and expressions, from his way of bringing you up short during maneuvers with swift, wordless gestures of a finger pointed towards instruments or stabbing outwards towards the far horizon or towards some invisible checkpoint in the skies; this for him was learning. Never, ever would this man have hinted that the time for your solo flight had come. Like everyone else, you prayed that it came between the sixth and eighth hour of dual-control training, otherwise, of this you were certain, it would never come at all.

Finally Bruno had climbed on board and you had begun to wait: to wait for him to place those schoolmasterly spectacles over his nose and to transcribe the initial data relating to the flight, to wait for that wave of the hand which meant switch on the engine and let's go, to wait for clearance from the tower to begin taxying, and then, once parked at the end of the runway, clearance for lineup and takeoff. Waiting was as much part of flight as flying itself, waiting, checking and double-checking; there is always some worthwhile means of filling in waiting time, there is always something on board to be attended to in the final moments before you push the lever and bounce slowly forward, and, thinking it over now, you should have had seen to it then. When the cosmic order of things, or the concatenation of events or the sheer force of coincidence had finally arranged themselves for liftoff, there you were applying power, releasing the brakes, staring at the rev counter and the anemometer, using the pedals to control the aircraft's right-left yawing movements. The run-up to takeoff is a metamorphosis: here is a pile of metal transforming itself into an airplane by the power of the air itself, each takeoff is the birth of an aircraft, this time like all the others you had had the same experience, the same wonder at each metamorphosis. Towards the end of the metamorphosis and of the runway, you feel the airplane surging upwards, no longer a creature of earth; too many leaps, too much yawing this way and that, you can no longer keep it on earth, better fly than race like this, your part is simply to wait for it to become an airplane, to wish that the transformation had already occurred; at that point, it sometimes rises up under its own force, calming itself as it rises, at other times it needs just a gentle, very gentle invitation from the control column. You had issued the invitation with delicacy, the merest millimeter so as not to wrench the plane roughly from earth, then you had casually pulled one more time, as though repeating a word spoken too low and unheard. You pulled gently but the plane did not respond. You gave a longer pull but the plane declined to follow you. You pulled firmly but still the plane did not lift off. You had looked out onto the runway and realized that you were more than halfway down its length, you saw the strip of sea beyond the mouth of the harbor, look at how it's rushing towards you, no, look at the dashboard and the dials, concentrate! and you went over the instruments one by one, as though pleading with each of them to side with you in some street brawl, and they did, everything was all right, but still the aircraft refused to leave the ground. Without turning around, you sought out Bruno's profile, a profile carved in stone, arms crossed, gaze unflinching, as though waiting: but there was nothing to wait for, the runway was ending, the aircraft was not lifting and you no longer had sufficient room to brake. Concentrate yet more intensely, stare at the instrument panel, stare harder, and by the sheer effort of staring you finally spot it: that's what was wrong, how could you have missed it? The flaps had not been released, the flap lever was still up, flap maneuver zero, you had forgotten the flaps. There must be some forty meters of runway remaining, not a centimeter more, then the sea; you had endeavored to slip your hand from the engine control to the flaps without Bruno noticing, you had desperately struggled to lower that lever, the end of the runway perilously close, your left hand still clutching the column, the right almost furtively giving the lever a sharp blow. Such was the accumulated speed that the moment the flaps began to descend from the trailing edge of the wings, the plane was sucked up, seized bodily, raised from the earth as though liberated, wrenched up above the embankment at the end of the runway, above the harbor mouth, above the bay and out over the sea.

Bruno's silence had immediately appeared to you a matter of concern; better say something. You had said, *We* forgot the flaps, in an offhand tone, with an ironic plural which implicated him in the oversight, even though he would never have forgotten the flaps; you were at the controls and it was entirely your responsibility, as well you knew. Bruno made no answer and you continued your ascent while waiting for further orders. After takeoff he would announce the flight plan, the items which might feature on today's menu:

stalls and spins? sharp turns? navigation? engine trouble? radar approach to an airport? But Bruno uttered not a word, nothing, not the merest glance; he did no more than make a wide circular gesture with one hand, a downward, spiralling movement which conveyed a swerve over the sea, a rapid return to the island, an immediate landing. The gesture's abruptness suggested that for you the landing would be definitive and permanent. So that was the plan.

The fear of a short time previously, the fear of the runway coming to an end was as nothing compared to the desolation of the present, when even your soul seemed to be blushing; had it been possible, you would have got out there and then, in midair, leaving him to take charge of the airplane; your next hope was to make at least a dignified farewell with a good landing, or more precisely a perfect landing, the sort of masterpiece of a landing that would have shown him what you were capable of; but on the final approach, over the trees which seem inexplicably to ring every airfield, you ran into a spot of turbulence: slight shudder of the airplane, immediate correction, landing on one wheel, bounce, land again, further bounce, land. You made straight for the hangar, you simply wanted to get there as quickly as possible, but just as you were turning onto the taxiway, you had felt a resistance on the pedals; I can't even turn on land, you said to yourself, when it occurred to you that Bruno had his foot on the pedal on his side and was making the plane pull up at the side of the runway. What was wrong now? You had cut the revs so low that the propeller was barely turning. Bruno had given you a rapid glance, then looking at you more squarely had said, How do you feel about going up on your own?

Don't pretend, you understood perfectly, the whole thing happened only a few moments ago; of course you understood perfectly, but had to run the entire gamut of emotions before regaining your balance, and even then you needed another pause before getting sufficient grip on yourself not to appear too delighted or too smug. You were then able to reply, Yes, if you're sure, why not? Bruno switched on the radio, asked the tower to suspend the traffic over the airfield, explained the reason why. Then he turned to you and said, You do know it's going to be a bit different, it will take off more quickly, climb much faster, I'll be standing here at the edge of the airfield, make all your calls to me as though you were talking to the tower. He gave you a last look as though you were an item on the final checklist, taking in what was showing on your face, the controls, the fastened safety belts, the cockpit. He even stopped as he climbed down to check that the door was properly closed.

On your own, here you are on your own, the solo pilot, as it will be recorded in the aeronautical registers. The word "solo" makes you sound like a violinist, when all you are is a person on your own inside an airplane in the middle of a runway, now speaking into the radio and communicating that you are lined up ready for takeoff, even if you still can't quite believe it yourself; lined up you undoubtedly are, but whether you are ready is another matter. Bruno replies "cleared" and reminds you of wind strengths, wind patterns and directions, but who's going to have time to think about the wind, to figure out where it's coming from and how strong it might be? In a moment or two there may be time, once you have pushed forward the levers and started to lift the soles of your feet from the pedals, then there may be time. The plane moves, quarter way down the runway you ask yourself why on earth Bruno ever decided to let you do it instead of kicking you out for good, halfway down you begin to feel tremors of something called responsibility, even if you are not clear whose, then gradually as the machine transforms itself into an airplane, you too transform yourself into Bruno and assume command of yourself, and in this new dimension you pull yourself together, check yourself and correct yourself as though you were a schoolboy. There are things to do, and these cancel out every other thought, and only after doing the things that needed doing, after closing the things that needed to be closed, opening the things that needed to be opened and regulating the things that needed to be regulated, only now that the plane has levelled out in the sky can you, in the light morning mist, look out over the sea and the horizon and see them for the first time not merely as reference points for checking turns, ascents and descents but as a landscape to which from now on you could belong, just as on earth you belong to the rivers and mountains.

You glide along the coast in a fantasy of immobility and timelessness, on the right the island, on the left the sea, you glide along thinking of the first time you made the ascent with Bruno, the first time, the orientation and test flight, preceding even the medical examination, you flew without putting a hand on the controls, seated on the right, relishing the panorama as Bruno soared calmly into the skies, at one point turning to you and asking if your seat belt was fastened properly, you had replied yes, offhandedly, and he pulled out his glasses, bent over a metal plate in the middle of the instrument panel where a notice in English indicated the aerobatic capability of the plane and, without lifting his hand from the control column, ran his fingers over the embossed lettering: no more than three spins, he read aloud, as though he did not already know that plane through and through, or as though it were essential for you to be made aware that after the third spin it was curtains; then, without a word, he had removed his glasses and sent the airplane careering into a nosedive, spinning as it went, without warning every part of you was pitched forward as you both plunged downwards still seated, the plane rotating on its axis, while down below the shoreline and the beach spun crazily round as they did in films, three spins he had said, but you seemed to have done thirty or three hundred already, I'm going to die with this man I don't know; but how were you to know then that Bruno was Bruno, that he had been an aerobatic pilot and a test pilot and that in the postwar years he had earned his living doing pirouettes at air shows, or that he had notched up thirty thousand flying hours on every type of plane. You prayed to God that this white-haired gentleman knew what he was about and that he had the skills to match, that the airplane would not disintegrate, that the dizzying, spinning plunge would stop at once.

It was no better the second time when, without more ado, he made you sit on the left, in the pilot's seat, no less! Out of the vast array of instruments, dials and electronic odds and ends that make up a control panel, he explained no more than the indispensable minimum before telling you to take off and head straight for the open sea. It was a grey, overcast day, and when that dense greyness had become one all-enveloping, impenetrable, hypnotic mass, Bruno turned to you quite suddenly with the words, Let's go back, where's the airfield? You glanced over your shoulder to look through the windows at the rear, but the view behind was the same as the view ahead, grey and more grey as far as the eye could see, with not a speck of land in sight, nothing which was in any respect distinguishable from that terrifying, flat, blinding calm. You in your turn asked, Yes, exactly, where is the airfield? Bruno shrugged his shoulders. You're in charge, he said, it's up to you to know these things and get us home. To start with, you swung to the left, purely out of intuition, for then you knew next to nothing about compasses or back courses, and all those position-finding instruments were a closed book to you. Guided by nothing more than a memory of the space and an instinctive orientation, you turned left and left again, and when it seemed you had gone far enough you straightened up. You turned to Bruno in the hope of some sign of assent or dissent, but were rewarded with another shrug. You ploughed on in the greyness, leaning forward against the windscreen so as to see better, to guess the lie of a coast, but there was no trace of any coastline; you peered in every direction but nowhere was there any sign of land until, in the all-encompassing greyness, a greyer, finer and more distant line appeared; it was the coast, but what coast, and at which point? Well done, you had sighted land, but the airfield was not there, nor was the city nor even the lagoon. You were too far to the south. When the coast took on the feel of a real landscape, Bruno gave directions with the gestures of a camel driver. In future, he said, when you take off remember to make a note of the position, if you intend going back, that is.

Bruno's voice on the radio now asks you to come in to land; the first solo landing is, of necessity, the reverse of the first solo takeoff, and God help you if it were otherwise! Bruno's voice on the radio always has a touch of uncertainty and concern, as once you had occasion to notice in the control tower, listening in with an operator. Bruno sidles cautiously up to words as though coming from somewhere he prefers not to name, giving the impression that words are the last resort when all alternatives have failed. On this occasion, the tone is deeper and the worry greater, perhaps because the trees at the bottom of the runway block his sight of you, and from the ground he asks your position in strict aeronautical jargon, and immediately afterwards asks in everyday language if everything is OK, and you give the position in aeronautical jargon and reply yes, everything's fine. And finally, while you go through the downwind checks, while you remove the antifreeze and enrich the mixture and cut back on engine speed and set the flaps at ten degrees, finally it occurs to you that the first takeoff is the meeting of two fears—yours and his, the mutual, shared fears of two people obliged to face the one event with only partial knowledge. What does Bruno know about you? Nothing at all. Mere intuition. Has he ever witnessed your hysterical scenes? Your moments of total abstraction? Has he ever seen you experience those moments of rapture, when you lose yourself in a void and leave behind your body like yesterday's newspaper to fill a spot you have vacated? Or those moments of ice-cold, bitter, deaf rage or pure hatred—those forces of evil to which you would so happily give vent? And what would Bruno say if he knew that leaving the airfield in the evening and walking home, you enjoyed keeping time to ditties of your own composition, like:

> The night has arrived
> The planes are asleep
> The tower is dark
> The fax makes a bleep

If you were in Bruno's shoes, would you entrust a plane to a man like that? What can have made him believe you were up to it, what does Bruno know about you? Only what he may have deduced from a very limited area, such as piloting a plane, an aptitude and activity which can, admittedly, be subject to scrutiny, but for the rest, for all the other things about a person, the things that matter and would matter more than anything else in those crucial moments of midair emergency, he can only go by intuition and deduction from those acts, those few acts he has seen you carry out; this is the risk he is running, what if there were engine trouble right now? An engine has no way of knowing who is at the controls, chance never takes circumstances or a pilot's experience into consideration. The other person, who just happens to be you, ought to have adequate self-knowledge, or at least that's the hope, but who can say if he really has that grasp of aeronautics, that pilot's know-how which at this moment of his life, on his first solo landing, now seem to him so crucial, and it's here that your greatest risk lies. As the final turn to the left brings the city into view, with the island on the right and the airfield straight ahead, speak into the radio, call on final, flaps out, landing gear down, landing lights. There's Bruno, a tiny figure standing on the grass border of the runway, looking upwards, walkie-talkie clasped to ear, That's just fine, he murmurs, just fine, you repeat to yourself, checking distance and trim. You are sitting on an accumulated inheritance of speed and height waiting to be dissipated and run down, the descent is the richest moment of flight (the body is the prime gauge of this wasting bonanza, of this wealth dispersed in descent and free fall, of the pure joy of refound weight and gravity), drop the nose of the aircraft, let it go, let yourself go, come down in a gentle glide over the trees, if you were not so tense and concentrated you would notice the shadow projected ahead of you by the sun at your back and could watch it expand on the grass and touch down a few moments ahead of you, your shadow has landed, your plane following it down, let yourself go, place the central wheels on the grass and for a moment keep the aircraft suspended in that position, a moment later the nosewheel touches down, leaving you only to brake, gradually, decisively, to brake until the thing carrying you, on which you are seated, slows down and ceases to be an airplane.

All that's left is to make your way to the hangar, *taxi to park,* the last maneuver cleared by Bruno over the radio before handing you over to the control tower, now that the airfield has reopened for traffic; it may be simply a clearance to backtrack off the runway, but in your mind it is a clearance of vast import, the first step in an enterprise just beginning and which could be ended only by some terminal event, an overriding clearance bringing with it many small, accompanying clearances, like the clearance to receive less severe treatment from the mechanic standing there, crossed forearms aloft—the sign for flight terminated, engines off, complete stop—at the end of the yellow line you are meticulously following with the nosewheel.

(If there existed some compartment of the memory reserved for first times, you think as you check that everything is switched off, you would place first takeoff alongside first lovemaking, for the intensity of the two is identical, however curious it may seem that for you the first and most overwhelming fusion with another human being should be put on the same level as the first and most total loneliness of all—the utter solitude of the solo pilot.)

And, when you climb out of the cockpit, there can be numbered among the innovations that distant hint, if not exactly of a smile at least of a less glowering expression from Bruno, accompanied by a new informality of address that betokens friendship, but an informality which in no way reduces the distance between the two of you, quite the reverse, and which does not alter his general demeanor, even if later in his office—if "office" is the right word for a forties desk, a rack of aeronautical maps, a rocking chair and a monitor showing a cloud-covered Italy as seen at this moment from a meteorological satellite—this tentative informality will permit you, while that instructor himself, dressed in his unvarying captain's uniform of dark tie over white shirt, sits down to put his signature to your first solo takeoff, to take advantage of this newfound confidentiality and ask why today precisely, why this morning of all mornings when you had just forgotten the flaps and came near to ending up in the sea; and will permit him, with a rapid, puzzled glance, to reply to you—Why today? plainly incredulous that you have not grasped. The mistake, because of the mistake, you saw the mistake yourself. The tone is offhand, whispered, as though he were repeating something obvious and, more importantly, secret. When else? he concludes, handing you back your logbook.

As soon as you are outside, you stop in the slanting light of the morning and leaf through the pages, searching out the handwriting, the signature which definitively enrolls you in the halls of celestial error, where each error is a scar, but not one which will ward off further relapses.

Between Second 1423
and Second 1797

NIGHT FELL ON the airfield. The mechanics, Bruno, the men in the control tower, even the woman behind the bar, they had all gone off leaving me alone with the runway lights, those bluish, glowing insects standing silently in unbroken lines in the grass. I stared at the shadows thrown by the tables onto the moonlit terrace, I stared at the night, the boundless horizons of night, at sea and sky separated only by streaks of light on far-off coastlines, and felt myself guardian of this nocturnal space. They had left me the key to the control tower, with orders to switch off the runway lights before leaving. Never had I lingered so long. The August night glided in humid heat towards its most intimate heart. Perhaps it was the heat, or perhaps I dozed off. One minute more, I thought, one minute more and then I'll get up and go, one minute more and I'll get up, switch everything off and leave; and perhaps I really would have. I was just on the point of rising to my feet when I became aware of their presence, two of them, seated a little way ahead of me in the darkness, how had I not seen them before now? I thought it might be no more than an image of my mind, but the sound of a voice, conveying the certainty that there really was someone there, sent a shiver down my spine.

"If only the weather had been like this that evening," said the younger man, "if only there had been this moon, this stillness..." Then he took his eyes from the sky, lowered his head and turned to me, and I, with a fresh shudder, made out his eyes in the darkness.

The other, the older man, looked first one way and then the other, as though anxious to find his bearings and, picking at the nail of one hand with a fingernail from the other, gave the impression that speaking required an effort and suffering beyond all endurance.

"Now," said the younger man, "now at last, we can measure the time which flashed past so rapidly that evening, a time of utter bewilderment, the bewilderment with which you said at the final moment, 'We're going to crash...' You spoke without yelling, in a voice choked by the pressure, the gravity which was tugging us down, as though resigned to that unbelievable thing which was taking place, an incident of such stupidity, such banality as an ice stall. You were captain, I was copilot, and apart from age what separated us was your greater familiarity with jets and mine with propellers..."

"Yes, I was captain," said the older man, "but you had taken over for that stretch, and I only came in at the end, but it doesn't matter now, believe me, it just doesn't matter."

"At second 1423," the younger man began again, "you told the hostess to give out the meals to the passengers, don't you remember? You spoke in a jovial tone, everything was going fine, there was no turbulence. 'When you get to the coffee,' you said, 'bring me a coffee with sugar.' You also asked her if there was an extra tray for us, and she replied that there was just the right number of trays but perhaps one of the passengers wouldn't want anything to eat, and you said that if there was only one left over it was for me."

"Strange, did we really talk so much about food?" said the older man, shaking his head gently.

"Yes, we discussed food, then at second 1492, when the plane was set on its ascent towards the Alps, you said, 'Let's get a bit of rest,' and it must have been more or less in those seconds that we passed the exact point where another plane ahead of us had turned back because of the ice, but how were we to know? We were tuned in to a different frequency and there was no way we could pick up its communications. We continued our ascent, and it was at second 1653 that I became aware that something was going wrong, we were losing lift and speed; the same thought occurred to both of us, we both immediately thought of ice. I switched on the wing lights and peered out to see where it was forming. I asked you if you didn't think it was along the trailing edge of the wing, and you replied Yes, it's over there, look. Ice crystals, the worst of all aeronautical ices, an ice which, the moment you enter a cloud, forms as swiftly as a blow to the face, difficult to shake off, molten water in the inside of a cloud, water which retains its liquid state

even in subzero temperatures, invisible particles in unstable equilibrium which remain raindrops only because a film of water envelops each single drop and
stops it from freezing, but the very instant something
collides with the film and breaks it open, the drops
solidify around whatever shattered them. We've
ploughed into a cloud at two hundred and seventy
kilometers an hour, we must have shattered millions,
billions of water drops which will have immediately
solidified and clung to the wings like barnacles to a
ship's hull. We're loaded down with ice crystals, it's
changed the shape of the wings, as well as their
weight. At second 1740, you told me to up the speed
by another four knots, or else we'd never make it, and
I did, but at second 1748 there was a sudden lurch of
the wing on my side, all of a sudden the plane tilted
over by forty degrees, maybe a bit less; it felt like a
sharp turn. I immediately disconnected the automatic
pilot and took manual control of the plane. It was all
done so quickly you didn't even notice me do it. You
said, 'Switch off autopilot,' and I said, 'I've already
done it.' At second 1750, the stall warning sounded. I
was struggling to keep the plane steady, but it was
already starting to lose height, and then the wing went
down on your side. A one-hundred-degree tilt to the
left, one hundred degrees...do you have any idea of
what that means?" asked the younger man, turning
to me. "It means a wing hanging like a knife blade,
a passenger aircraft cutting the air like a knife," and
he shook his head in dismay. "At second 1755, I felt
a jolt in the instruments as the automatic mechanism
came into play, pushing the control column forward

with forty-kilo pressure to counteract the stall. I shouted out Down...down...down, and you shouted Steady...steady...steady, and took over the controls. We stalled one more time, the third; this time it was the wing on my side, another hundred degrees to the right; you cursed the plane at the top of your voice, you screamed, 'God damn you,' I remember it very clearly..."

The captain listened as though he had gone over those seconds a million times. "Do you hear him?" he asked me, adjusting the brim of his cap, "do you hear how he speaks about them? 1492, 1653, 1748, as thought they were years, historical dates, but we're talking about barely three hundred seconds, five minutes; five minutes, that's all the time we had to grasp what was going on, to come to grips with things, to tack desperately, one night in early autumn, caught in a mass of never-ending clouds, in a sky of terrible ice. That's all there is to it, we do nothing else, we have remained united even after the crash. He won't give himself peace, and yet we stuck to the manual, doing exactly what it said, but you see what he's like. Maybe it's because he's young, and young he's going to remain, forever."

All three of us fell silent, a silence broken by the cicadas and the warm heaving of the sea. We looked over towards the airfield; standing there with that moon overhead and those trees round its sides; with its thirties-style terminal building and old, steel half-barrel-vaulted hangars, the abandoned Fascist warehouses on the far side of the runway, its grass runway and double row of lights running down to the sea, it

could have been any airstrip, any airfield at any point
in the world where sea and land meet, waiting for any
takeoff or any landing, in any of the years and decades
of this, the first century of aviation, the site of every
departure and arrival, every cancelled departure, every
arrival awaited in vain.

Then, the young man in uniform began to speak
again. "Then at second 1760 the wing on my side
dropped down once again, you ordered me to cut back
the engines and I did, at second 1764 the stall warning
sounded yet again, the wing on your side stalled for
the umpteenth time, this time as much as one hundred
and thirty-five degrees, leaving the plane almost completely upside down, just imagine, a passenger plane
in inverted flight—" sighed the young man, gesticu-
lating with his hands, turning the palm of one hand
upwards then letting it go limp "—you and I were
upside down as well, and I don't know how, but with
the blood racing in my head and everything dancing
around me, I managed to make out the anemometer
among the flashing lights on the control panel, the
speed was climbing from one hundred and eighty-five
to two hundred and thirty-one knots, very slowly the
tilt was righting itself, the wing stalls stopped and I
thought to myself, Maybe we're going to make it,
maybe we can pull out of it, we attempted to regain
control by raising the nose ever so gently, although the
plane was still burbling a bit, it was second 1771, I
yelled to you, 'Haul it up…haul it up…,' and you
shouted back, 'I am hauling it up,' at that moment we
went over two hundred and fifty knots, the maximum
operational speed, triggering the overspeed alarm as

well. At second 1779, you said again, 'I am hauling';
but we were plummeting, over three hundred and
thirty knots, the upper limit of maneuverability, and
you shouted, 'The controls have jammed on me!' At
second 1787, you shouted once again, 'Pull hard,' and
I replied that I was pulling hard, the stall signals, the
overspeed signals, everything was blaring, everything
was vibrating and falling around us, and at that point,
God knows where I got the strength in that position
and at that speed, it was second 1789, I got onto the
radio and screamed, 'Milano, Alitalia Four Six Zero,
emergency...,' as though that message could have
saved us, as though anyone could have done anything
for us, or for the plane; I knew we'd lost her, I knew
we were lost, and yet it was unbelievable, we were
done for but it was at that very moment, second 1797,
that you said to me quietly, with that choked voice of
yours, 'We're going to crash,' and your voice was
quiet, sad and bewildered, 'We're going to crash...' "

"The following second..."

"Please," said the captain, "please," but he spoke as
though reciting a ritual prayer he did not expect to be
heard, it wasn't so much that he had no inclination to
hear one more time the hubbub of those final moments as that, perhaps, he wished to calm his first
officer, or perhaps did not want him to relive that final
instant, wanted it banished forever from his mind, a
futile prayer, because the following moment the
younger man began again in the same tone, he said,
"It was impossible to see a thing, we were falling at
the rate of ten thousand feet a minute, I first noticed
that something was the matter with the plane at

second 1653, but at second 1797, less than two minutes later, it was no longer an airplane, we were just fifteen thousand kilos of scrap metal, fibers, plastic and people, almost overturned, tumbling into nothingness, in the thick darkness of a cloudy night, quite helplessly, with no knowledge of what had occurred, or how. Can you imagine such a thing? We had collided with a cloud, we had rammed into a cloud which a few seconds later, intact and lighter by some few pounds of ice, would proceed peacefully on its way towards the east and which would, the morning after, when they found us lying among the trees, be floating heedlessly over the Ionian Sea or over the Balkans."

There was another silence, I considered making the effort to overcome my fear and take the first officer by the hand, what could happen to me? It would have been a gesture of solidarity and for that reason, I thought to myself, Someone, Nature or the Cosmos would exempt me from any horror and from all consequences, but the captain read the gesture in my eyes and, shaking his head gently, made a sign to desist. "Are you here every evening?" he asked, changing tack. "You're lucky, you know, it's a lovely spot, especially at this time, in this season," he said, adjusting the brim of his cap and gazing around with infinite, wistful nostalgia. After a moment, he said, "Could I have a look at the aircraft in the hangar?" "I'm sorry," I replied, "I'm really sorry but I don't have the keys. I've only got the keys to the control tower to switch off the runway lights." "Pity," said the captain, getting to his feet. The young officer rose too, as did I.

We walked towards the tower, unhurriedly, each

man caught up in his own thoughts, everything that could happen had already happened, terribly and irrevocably happened, and this certainty, together with the beauty of the place and the moonlight, seemed to imbue each of us with a total sense of oneness with the landscape, an utter acceptance of what is, as it is.

Even the tone of the younger officer had become more tranquil and distant, he was walking forward with hands deep in his pockets and his eyes fixed on the grass. "We plunged into a cloud," he was saying, "and we never emerged again, there was no chance of understanding anything, the only thing I could understand was that you were determined to keep climbing higher and higher, to break through the clouds as though you were piloting a jet, to give it more power and get clear, while I was anxious to descend and pick up speed, as you would do with a propeller plane. Who would have guessed that we would have gone back to propeller-driven planes in the run-up to the year 2000? And yet we did everything by the book, never deviating one iota, we followed the manual to the letter, so there must have been a mistake or something missing," said the young man, staring me straight in the eyes. The captain answered for me. "What's the point of going over it?" he asked in tones of ritual consolation. "With that ice we could never have made it, whatever we did, severe ice conditions, ice crystals, believe me, no one could ever have pulled out of it."

("Do you know," said the younger man, "I've often wondered what they think when they listen to the voices of dead pilots in the voice recorder, the one of the two black boxes which picks up what is said in the cockpit." "I used to know someone who did that job," said the captain. "He was an old flight engineer who had retired but carried on working with investigation teams who looked into airline accidents. I once asked him if it didn't upset him to listen to those voices, and he said, 'No, why?' 'But what do you expect to find that's not already in the flight recorder, in the record of the various flight maneuvers?' 'I'm interested in the tone of the voices,' he said, 'that's what matters, the tones of voice.'")

In the buoyed approach channel, a passenger ship festooned with colored lights shining brightly in the night was gliding, slowly and noiselessly, out from the harbor towards the open sea. All three of us stopped to stare at this majestic, imperturbable moving shadow framed by its own lights. "Did you hear the passengers behind us?" asked the younger man. The captain, with his eyes still fixed on the ship, nodded. "During the last moments," he said, "in the dying moments, I became aware of what they really were, those noises, those voices coming through our closed doors, and not only the voices. But only at the very last..."

At the foot of the control tower, feeling guilty at not being able to allow them into the hangar, I turned back and invited them to come up, but the captain, after a moment's hesitation, said, "No, I'm very grateful, but better not."

"I understand," I said, "just give me a minute and I'll be back down," I looked at the older man in his uniform and, raising his shoulders ever so slightly, he said, "Of course." A second later I bounded up the stairs four at a time, went into the darkened room, located the switch by the light of the moon which came flooding in through the great windows, bathing the small, circular room and instrument panels in its light; I pulled down the lever and the two rows of blue lights in the grass disappeared into the night, a road dissolving into the darkness; I thought, Even the runway goes to sleep, and one instant later I was rushing down the steps, another second and I was out on the path. I looked around, with no idea of what second it was, but they were nowhere to be seen. I raced over the grass, towards the trees, towards the hangar, towards the terrace, and finally I caught sight of them making their way along the unlighted runway, slowly, in the distance, their backs to me, one of them debating with himself, cutting the air with his hand, or turning the palms of his hands upwards, while the other, the older of the two, seemed to be keeping him company, but his face was turned away, towards the moon and the liner out at sea. I stood watching them until they faded into the dawn, the sea, the sky.

And Everything Else?

AS AN AVIATOR, I came from the street. I had behind me a long career as a walker; I had always walked a lot, almost always with my eyes fixed on the ground. I was hypnotized by movement, by the flow of the landscape in miniature. Since boyhood, it had always seemed to me that walking and staring at the ground reproduced the impressions available from an airplane: everything was in the correct proportion, even the speed seemed right, while the joins between paving stones could be roads surrounding housing developments, puddles could be volcanic lakes, and trickles of water in the gutter rivers in full spate with their tributaries. At an earlier stage, as a younger child, I imagined I was a tram and as I walked along a street, I would pull up at every stop, open and shut the doors with a puff of breath from between clenched teeth. When I was not engaged in urban rail transport, I felt like an airplane; not a pilot, I must insist, but an airplane. As an adult, I would make an even bigger airplane, a four-engined job, with an increase in wingspan and horsepower. As an airplane I was born from a tram, like a butterfly from a caterpillar, and as an airplane, even if I loved to skim my cheek along the ground in long, muddy swoops, I flew over the streets at a fixed altitude, the altitude of a child's eyes. As an airplane, I felt full responsibility for everything I was transporting, be they pilots, passengers, mail or poultry, and this sense of responsibility, for one like me who felt himself substantially a *thing,* belonging to the family of things, made me feel, as a thing, on a par with the living beings I had on board. Childhood is, among other things, a certain altitude, a certain relationship with the earth, a question of dimensions which will never again be experienced in life, a point of view held with tenacity which, once lost, will fade from memory leaving no trace. Nothing, except perhaps the wild extremes of violence or madness, will ever be able to restore to me that intimacy with gusts of dust, with blowing paper and insects, with the berries, roots and clay from which I come. It may be that in transforming myself into an airplane, I merely wished to be an adult, because only an illusion of continuity allows us to believe that the child and the adult who emerges from the child are one and the same, two stages of an identical unity; childhood does not develop, it simply falls away like milk teeth, to be replaced by a blend of a new substance, a compound of enamel and ivory, similar but never identical. The child and the adult are two divergent breeds in nature, different in species and classification (if in nothing else than in that underdeveloped determination to survive which leaves the child exposed to any risk, and that

pigheaded determination to survive which leaves the
adult exposed to any ridicule). So the tram that was
in me died away to be replaced by a reconnaissance
or transport child, formed from a bicycle prone to
crazy tilts to one side, to breakneck descents and falls:
a fighter-bomber of a child who forged relations with
friends based on their knowledge of the various makes
of airplane and of their functions, a knowledge culled
from a book of aircraft outlines as seen from earth.
The book, not dissimilar to many such manuals once
used in ornithology for the identification of birds in
flight, was presumably a leftover from the War which
I had picked up somewhere or other. The successive
moment, when I had to transmogrify from plane to
pilot, coincided with a painful phase of my life caused
in part by that metamorphosis itself, as well as by the
transition from being a bystander to being a partici-
pant. I had learned from the open-air cinema we attended in summer that there was a dignity to being a
bystander. At an early stage, I realized that heroes died
and theirs was the glory, but their friends and peers
preserved the memory, transmitted news of their
deeds, and theirs was the more serviceable part. I
found myself nurturing greater and greater sympathy
for these secondary, ever-present figures who took part
in the tragic action, knowing from the outset that it
would all finish badly, and whose actions made the
film possible: in their supporting role they gave a certain solidity to the whole affair. In the course of one
of those summer seasons, I decided that when I was
grown up, I would take the part of the bystander, even
if I found it difficult to say in exactly which field of

life. But there, in the same cinema, my airplane vocation was consolidated, and these were the only two paths that opened before me—airplane or bystander.

Becoming a pilot, then, meant abandoning a dual nature to which I owed allegiance, my airplane nature and my bystander nature; but there must be some lingering trace of my previous metallic stage, if even today I would prefer to attempt a crash landing rather than eject, and could never abandon an airplane to its fate. In any case, a mania is a mania, with time it is possible to see it at work, to decipher its continuity, to recognize how it operated underground, when it made its appearance, how it was hidden, justified, reformed and transformed into something else, silenced only to speak out in a different idiom; in self-defense, if self-defense is needed, I can only say that mind and mania have a common derivation.

The best kind of flight is undoubtedly flight of the mind; it requires no sophisticated means of transport, no license or qualifying exams, nothing other than the capability to be one's own pilot, the pilot of one's own imagination. For thousands of years, there was no other kind; the skies of antiquity were thick with air traffic, alive with multitudes of flying creatures or aero-objects which, were I to sight them now on the far side of my windscreen, I would be obliged to enter in official documents under the heading Unidentified Flying Objects—eagles controlled by winches, mechanical doves, or the aerial throne of Ka'us, a king who flew as far as the borders of China on board a four-engined seat, i.e., drawn by four eagles, pursuing four unattainable lambs' legs. I relished this attention

to the minute details of motorization, as though imagination were not of itself sufficient, but required the
underpinning of plausible mechanics; but this was, I
imagined, the means by which some premonition of
the dawn of the machine, or a longing for it, had
lurked inside the dream. Down the centuries, the only
pilot was the bard, and later the scribe, when he set
himself to recount the flights of Solomon or of
Muhammad, or of any of the earlier prophets who
set forth astride some aeronautical packhorse; the title
of pilot belonged also to anyone who recounted the
tale of Malek commanding the flying chest which de-
scended at the touch of one screw, ascended at the
touch of another and turned right or left at the touch
of yet others. Better still were the shamans, sufis and
all those who took to the air without any visible means
of support, trusting their souls to fly for them and to
continue searching on their behalf. Hundreds of
nameless pilots had flown as best they could, attrib-
uting wings to all that they saw in movement in space,
to the sun, the moon, the celestial bodies, then to the
gods, to animals and men, and then again to griffins,
dragons and all manner of nature's hybrids. Finally
there came the period of objects, and at that point
everything took to the air—carpets, sofas, hats, boots,
capes, rings, beds and all kinds of household imple-
ment. Honor and glory to those aviators of the mind
and imagination, scarcely a one of whom had to face
injury or pain, the only conceivable breakdown being
a failure of the imagination. As for me, in the course
of my metamorphosis from airplane to pilot, I lost my
ability to grow excited over the dove of Archytas of

Tarentum, over Bellerophon astride Pegasus or over that ship of Lucian of Samosata which was raised up by a gust of wind, hoisted from the sea and hurtled towards the moon. I loved Ovid, but the vision of Perseus soaring through the air with the head of Medusa dripping blood left me aeronautically cold, as did Daedalus and Icarus—the tale of the feathers detaching from the boy as the wax melted, leaving him flapping his wings in midair and falling into the sea, and of the father flying low over the waves but seeing nothing but scattered feathers. Leopardi had raised one devastating objection: how could the wax have melted if the greater the altitude, the lower the temperature? There was nothing more typical of Leopardi than that simultaneous attachment to myth and to the vertical thermal gradient. For me, the best of tales remained the tale of Simon Magus, the man who, in his keenness to impress the Roman people and please Nero, accepted the challenge of repeating Icarus' flight in public; with an apparatus of wings of his own devising, he presented himself to Saint Peter, and said to him, "Look here, Peter, in the sight of all these watching multitudes, I'm off to see the Lord in heaven," and Peter straightaway withdrew, knelt down on the stones of the Via Sacra and, raising his eyes to the sky where Simon Magus' prodigious deed was about to unfold, invoked the name of Christ: "Lord, of your grace, show your power to all those who are gathered here; I do not seek his death but merely request that his intestines be churned up a bit, that he fall to the ground and break his tibia in three places." I was entranced by the precision of the request for the fracture, by the fact that we were dealing with a little incident of black magic practiced by the Apostle Peter at the expense of Simon Magus: the fracture may have been on a demonist and simonist, but the real sorcerer was Peter and the victim Simon Magus, who stalled in midair, fell to the ground and died a few days later of a broken leg.

As an airplane, I belonged to the century of the switch to things, the most realistic century there has ever been, a century which has solidified fantasies into objects (and which later still, surpassing itself, would become the century of the disappearance of things and their replacement by images). For every myth unrealized by history, for every dream or simple fantasy narrative, this century would sooner or later set about constructing the physical object which was its perfect material incarnation, even if the means have been more wearisome, mechanical and graceless. *What is going on? Up there, twenty meters above ground level, a man imprisoned in a wooden cage is defending himself against an invisible danger to which he has voluntarily exposed himself:* I used to read this surprising sentence, here we have an airman of the mind taking the first photograph of an aircraft in the sky, an event imagined for thousands of years, predicted down to the details of the wood of the chest or cage, and which was no sooner made possible than distorted into a mechanical, inexplicable and absurd shape; the "imprisoned" pilot was Blériot, the "photographer" Franz Kafka. It was the first time Kafka had seen a man actually fly, and also the first time he had seen Gabriele D'Annunzio, while for D'Annunzio that af-

ternoon in 1909 in Brescia was the first time someone
had taken him flying. An afternoon of remarkable
firsts. And an afternoon of non-encounters. Kafka saw
and described D'Annunzio—a waddling little man—
but D'Annunzio paid no heed to Kafka, nor would
he have had any reason for so doing, since Kafka was
at the time merely a young man from Prague, unpub-
lished and unknown.

The crowds rushed to see the first aeronautical
demonstrations, and yet, I used to think, flight had
already been possible for more than a century, from
the age of the aerostatic balloon; but the aerostat never
seems to have satisfied people's expectations of flight,
perhaps on account of its immobility: a balloon in
equilibrium in the sky is anchored in the most complete inertia, possessing no movement of its own, the
balloon itself does not move, but is moved by the mass
of air to which it belongs. Everything around the aero-
naut is static, his cape does not billow, he does not feel
the action of the wind, not even when the gusts which
surround him drag him forward at high speed. If he
were to place some soap bubbles on a table in front of
him, they would remain in a state of absolute rest, a
candle flame would not flicker. A creature of an in-
terregnum, the aerostat was destined to remain suspended between the end of flight as myth and the
birth of flight as technical achievement; the curious
anchor which hung over the side of the basket indicated another of its amphibian, intermediate vocations,
as though, deriving from nautical associations with the
domain of fluids, there still existed some link with
the sea, with the liquid element; but unlike ships, the

aerostat could never take advantage of the dualism, of the air/water contradiction which permitted the mobility of ships and sails. The balloon was entirely a creature of the air, an air/air creature, forced to have its being inside one element only. It belonged more to the family of cloud than to the realm of flight.

That absence of wings in a flying object was intolerable to me. I had always linked flight with the winged form, probably because the winged creature is nature's model, it is the flying animal. Coming from a childhood as an airplane, I was well aware that machines concealed a secret rapport with the animal world, a contradictory relationship of assertiveness and power on the one hand but of imitation and nostalgia on the other, because although we had, through technology, liberated ourselves from that world once and for all, we had also separated ourselves from it once and for all. Names of models, of airplanes and of various other devices, often borrowed from the animal world or relating to it, could be produced in evidence: as a pilot, I would have occasion to fly in "falcons," "kites," and "storks," while the English term "cockpit," the pilot's cabin, retains an association with "poultry."

As an airplane, I had no idea why an airplane stayed airborne, nor indeed did I ever give it a second thought. Later, as a pilot, I was forced to recognize that although no one could explain why an airplane flies, and that it was easier to explain why it crashes, there were excellent rules which described the phenomenon, and precise laws detailing construction practice. I made an effort to attain some familiarity with these, and to acquaint myself with the speed which, bisecting the airflow, creates a depression on the upper side of the wing and builds up pressure on the underside, or those tiny air particles of the same flow line which divide on contact and wash round the wing, affording it both lift and support. Strangely, the lift and support are two-thirds produced by the depression on the upper part and only one-third by the pressure on the lower side, so that the plane is two-thirds lifted into the skies by suction and one-third supported—the only case in which depression, being stronger than all other forces, is uplifting. This is as much as can be said with certainty regarding flight.

Very quickly, a line was drawn between flight and *everything else.* I did what I could not to lose sight of *everything else,* but my self-image as a thing and as bystander sat awkwardly with the new consciousness of being a pilot which occupied my body like a pregnancy. I awaited the moment when it would become a straightforward aspect of my life, but that moment was slow to arrive, in part because I lived day and night in the airfield, an old airfield, and when I was not flying I was hobnobbing with the engineers or the people in the tower, sharing the maintenance work and helping out with the communications, and if there was a spare part to be picked up, a propeller to be taken somewhere or a radio to be repaired, I would climb aboard with the others and take off for Bolzano or Forlì. There were many advantages for me in this, because on one point there could be no doubt: everything was worthwhile, flight was a purely intellectual and cultural matter, the more you knew the greater were your chances of living, the more you knew, the better you would be at flying, and who could say in what sky, in what bank of clouds or in what emergency it would be of advantage to know, or to be able to pluck from your mind, how the camber of a wing was constructed, where the engine was positioned against the deckhead, where the rods ran which carried air to the navigation instruments, transforming that air, which already provided thrust and support, into meaning and orientation. But I must be more sincere: precisely because I had been a thing, I possessed a wholly natural insight into how things were made. I had an instinctive knowledge of the names of the parts, of how the parts were connected to the whole—to the entire whole—and although I had no idea where I had acquired this knowledge and vocation, I have always been ashamed of it, and continue to live with a deep sense of guilt and of waste on its account. Certainly, as Bruno would have agreed, instinct is fundamental, and there is no way it can be cultivated except through flying and more flying, if not in the skies then by "hangar flight," that is, "flight talk" in the sheds and yards, and immersion in everything which has anything to do with flight. Flight, and here was another piece of knowledge acquired early, was totally unnatural, indeed for us it is the most unnatural thing of all, while fear of it is a healthy, sane emotion. Flight had revealed its unnaturalness at the very moment when it ceased being flight of the mind to become an experience of the body; it was undeniable that even shamanistic or mystic flight contained a physical element, even if it was not altogether easy to probe its nature, at least not for me, obliged as I was, by my own inadequacy, to fly with a metal extension, piloting what I had once been. I had to express myself in terms of conducting, and found it oddly pleasing that the word "conduct" could refer either to the control of the craft or to moral character. To make flight "natural" it had been necessary to formalize it as far as possible, to draw up a complicated grammar of rules and exceptions, a body of procedures and precedents, corrected and emended over the decades in the light of errors and catastrophes, because errors in this grammar were paid cash, and at top prices. Every technical jargon, on its first appearance, distances itself from everyday language and received knowledge to construct its own lexicon of new words, mental images and autonomous spatial representations, and in so doing extends the limits of our knowledge and general language, and occasionally alters, at least in part, our style of living and dying. However, little by little, even a jargon used exclusively in one trade begins to give something back to vocabulary and common sense, probably at the moment of its maturity, or widest diffusion, or else at the beginning of its decline. It is as though it were freeing something which had been in custody inside it, hidden by its operation, perhaps ideas of behavior or orientation, emotions, or journeys of the mind or of perception. It is like a slow return to the mother tongue. It was this something which, in the act of breaking with my airplane nature, I began to call "the pilot's lore."

As a boy, I numbered among my possessions a *Guide des voyages aériens Paris-Londres*, another of those mysterious objects which came into my hands God knows how, certainly not from my parents who were never in any condition to contemplate air travel; the pamphlet was in any case published in the twenties when they would still have been children. It was a straightforward guide, at best a *"Guide officiel,"* as it stated on the cover, sold to the passengers on the first airline to make the crossing of the English Channel. For years I had been able to do no more than flick through the pages, spending hours poring over the photographs of cities, countryside and landscapes without understanding that those aerial views with captions like *"Un virage sur Paris!"* or *"La Plage du Crotoy,"* or *"La Comté de Kent"* were not merely illustrations to a text I could not read, but were, on the contrary, the very subject of the guide. The aim of the guide was to teach people how to see, and through seeing, how to follow the geography along the route, from the initial turn over Paris after takeoff at Ecouen, to the Lake of Enghien, the beach of Crotoy, the port of Boulogne, the Channel, then on to Ashford, Maidstone and finally the airport of London-Croydon. Pictures, in the days of my airplane childhood, were not particularly frequent, so a book with pictures had to last; the *Guide*, abandoned occasionally for brief periods, lasted for me beyond my adolescence, when I was finally able to understand the text, whose opening passage ran: "The passenger who goes up in an airplane for the first time will receive one surprise after another. His vision of the world will be revolutionized. Very quickly vertical vision will take over from the horizontal vision to which he has been accustomed all his life. The air traveller is at times completely lost in the air. The eye requires to be completely re-educated, but this task can be accomplished in a very brief time. Very soon, once you are able to put a name to the towns, to recognize squares and buildings or walk above cities, the monotonous mosaic of the fields will acquire a vivid life of its own. Vertical vision is a novelty because it reduces everything—mountains, monuments and even the Eiffel Tower—to a surface. But this vision is rare and fleeting. More commonly, it is oblique vision which comes as a shock to the eye. In this case, houses, monuments and raised points present themselves to you under a cubic appearance. But you will quickly adjust to oblique vision, which is, in all truth, more complete than vision of the surfaces."

As a pilot, I had the opportunity to test the truth of these lines, which for years I had commented on in silence, as though they were a psalm. The vision of any airman is not vision from above, vertical vision *"est rare et fugitive,"* in fact, for a pilot, vertical vision does not exist, to look down vertically below me, I would have needed a trapdoor or a porthole directly beneath my feet, like the bomb-aimer who sat in the belly of the plane precisely because he needed to cor-rect vertical vision. Besides, the only way I had of flying vertically over any landmark on the ground was to fly around it in a circle, choosing that point as the center of constant rotation, and keeping it continually within my sight range. A pilot's real vision was, as the *Guide* had stated at the outset, a *"vision oblique,"* not a vision from overhead: *"La vision à la verticale est rare et fugitive. Le plus souvent, c'est la vision oblique qui vous surprend. Alors les maisons, les monuments, les reliefs se présentent sous l'aspect cubique.*" I have no way of saying how much that "cubique" owed to the painting styles in vogue this century, or how much it had influenced them. I was content with its metaphorical meaning and overall implication; it would have been sad if the price of flight were a condemnation to the "vision of things from above," which is the property of the Divinity, and which would have induced in each of us a feeling not only of unworthiness, but also of downright embarrassment and dejection.

This was, however, a problem I became aware of as a pilot, but which previously, as a child-airplane, had not interested me in the slightest. The pilot's vision was a relationship with the earth and a relationship of spatial depth, with the link maintained primarily by an optic thread, the visual pencil of the perspective in which your eye was only one of the vertices, determined by all the others. I learned to take my position from that vision and correct the trim. The extent to which that visual link was accurate and essential to piloting was something I tested every day in the final approach to landing. The illuminated rods at the sides of the runway changed color depending on the point from which they were observed: if they appeared white, you were flying above the ideal glide path, if all red you were too low, and if you were at the correct level you saw the furthest off as red and those nearest to hand as white. From a distance, a genuine shining path presented itself to the eye; if I succeeded in coming in along that chromatic change, keeping the distant rods red and the nearer ones white, I would touch down at the correct contact point. All this in the best of circumstances.

Since the days I had ceased rubbing my cheek in puddles in face-to-ground landings, I had never again entered into such a necessary relationship with the earth. In spite of that, I began to wonder what I had gained and what I had lost in the passage from airplane to pilot. I had undoubtedly lost in terms of naturalness and joy; in the days of my thinglike nature as a piece of metal, I used to close my eyes and roll in ditches, rattling like a tin can without a care in the world, whereas now, as a pilot, much more thought was needed. In order to execute a half-roll in the skies, I had to calculate speed and height, and while rotating head down I had to keep my eyes on the instrument panel, and that loop which might from a distance seem to display grace and elegance required control, forethought and preparation, not to mention discussions after landing to make out why it had not worked for me. Where I had, perhaps, gained was in my relationship with *everything else*, or that at least was my hope. But probably I had come too late, and my metamorphosis had occurred in an age I would like to term the "twilight of the pilot." Airplanes, even ones which I piloted, were filled with electronic and automatic devices; it was clear to everyone that in the vast earth-air-earth system, the pilot, which was what I was girding myself to become, was to be considered the weak point, the point of breakdown. So I thought that I might perhaps have gained some sense of the complexity of the "pilot's lore," and so a more mature grasp of the variety of *everything else*, with its tangle of plots, its impossible choices, its polarities that tear you apart.

In flying, there were things to which I felt attracted by instinct, and many others—meteorology and orientation, mechanics and the airplane—with which I was familiar through having been part of them; there was also geography, which I loved as an art of location, and in that vision, be it oblique, cubic or whatever, space became representation. It became possible to experience the continuity which linked the plain to the mountains, the rivers to their dissolution in the deltas, the cities to their attrition in the suburbs, and even the history of human settlement presented itself as an immediate perception of necessity and decay; in flight, geography and history were united in the simultaneous portrayal of the perfect chaos to which we belong.

But there was yet more, even if I only came to understand it much later: flight, unnatural and artificial as it may be, had been an extreme threshold, a final border wherein by instinct or procedure one could travel through the infinite multiplicity of variables while maintaining trim; flight was an extreme dimension of probability, as narrow as the tiny margin of lateral or vertical tilt permitted to an airplane if it is to remain airborne. It had been possible to plough or cultivate this margin like a strip of land in the desert; the "pilot's lore" took this as its subject, the abiding subject, because this was also the subject of *everything else*. Except that the nature of everything else was changing, it was no longer sufficient to locate balanced wisdom at the extremes; the active part of government, of *conduct*, seemed no longer, or not exclusively, taken up with infinite, complex, unpredictable variables but with an eruption of afflictions as open as wounds or sneering mouths. The "pilot's lore" had a pliability, a suppleness and a complexity which derived from the dimensions involved, from the natural element on which it worked, the omnipresent, ever-elusive air with its terrifying laws. It demanded foresight and yet, at the same time, of its essence, of the nature of navigation, it needed total adaptability to circumstances; but in each of these contexts, whether dealing with clouds, route or some symptom of breakdown, in all this liquidity and multiplicity there was for each question one point around which that lore had to harden or solidify in an instant decision, one gesture which excluded all others. In the world of *everything else*, this moment was becoming obsolete, and I, in that world, had transformed myself from airplane to pilot precisely at the time of the twilight of the pilot, when not even the best of men could succeed in both keeping open the wounds and mending the pain.

Pauci Sed Semper Immites

AT DUSK, I used to sit at one of the tables in the old terrace bar, scarcely a terrace at all, more a slightly raised flooring of cracked tiles with a railing around the side; from there the whole deserted runway could be seen, the green of the grass clashing so stridently with the sea that only the hour and the season made the effect plausible. I killed time listening to the barmaid complain about her son who spent all his time in the hangars with the mechanics instead of giving her a hand, and in reply I sang the praises of the same mechanics and put up a stout defense of the highly educational value of their company. She paid no heed to me as she finished winding up the faded awning, locked the glass-panelled door from inside and went on her way in the company of those few who were still hanging about after all flights were in, which was when the airfield closed down. Having spent the day flying, I stayed on, with a beer and a manual; in the last flickering light, in the peace which preserved the memory of the flights, I despaired over the mistakes

I had committed and over all the things that were still beyond me. That evening my despair was related to the double three-sixty, a landing procedure for planes with engine trouble, consisting of a twin-spin, spiral descent with engines switched off, executed while losing so many feet in the first spin and the same number in the second, all the while keeping the airplane, which was no longer engine-driven, at the speed of maximum efficiency, the speed at which it would travel furthest, and at the same time mentally dividing the runway into three segments, deciding in a split second where to touch down with the wheels and then touching down at exactly that point. I would never get the hang of it.

"Do you really think it's that hard?" asked the elderly gentleman, sitting down at my table. "You should have seen what they made us do, believe me, nothing ever changes, the figures are still the same, this three and sixty of yours was attempted by Lindbergh in training at Brooks Field, San Antonio, that must have been, let me see, 1923 or '4, the figures are like dance steps, looping, *tonneau*—one, two, three, *pas de deux, pas glissé, pas floré*—always the same, by the way are you a dancer? Listen, it's important to be able to dance, I was pretty good at the Cuban Eights, which is not all that difficult, granted, but what a dance step to try in the skies. The same's true of the wing loop, which I used to do with a plane not exactly built for aerobatics. You know the one I'm talking about, the old Seventy-nine, the most famous of all Italian three-engined warplanes, a great hulking, ten-thousand-kilo beast."

I had not noticed the elderly gentleman before the bar shut, but now as the sun set slowly behind the row of trees, we were the only two left in the little airfield. The man fiddled with an eye-catching tie pin which, together with the handkerchief peeping out of the top pocket of his woollen summer jacket, gave him an air of ironic composure. He started up again: "You know what I used to do? I would set off flying so low as to be almost skimming the ground, ripping along at four hundred kilometers an hour, pull back, heavily at first then gradually releasing the control column, make the plane trace a parabola in the sky, take it right up to the top of the ascent, the point where it stopped climbing, and that's where you had to maneuver, not a second too soon nor a second too late if you wanted a perfect circle, just at the moment when you felt yourself hanging like a salami from the rafters and your mouth had gone bone dry and you were staring at an anemometer which was touching zero and the engines were spluttering because they couldn't climb any higher, then I'd grab the handle on the left and slam down the pedal on the same side and the Seventy-nine would turn on its left wing and go careering in a nosedive towards the earth. At that point, it was time to cut out the other two engines, the speed climbed madly, I jammed on the trim crank to reverse the descent and pulled at the control column, by God you should have seen me pull! With a long circular, descending arc, the plane found level flight, skimmed over the eucalyptus trees and came down low and smooth on the fields. The first time I tried it, I came near to killing myself, but I wanted to celebrate 'my'

Seventy-nine. 'Your plane is here, Martino,' said my
CO. I left the crew behind, except for my flight engineer, and the two of us went up together, but when
we were in the middle of that loop, our hearts were
in our mouths, I can tell you, it was a beautiful spring
morning in '42, I'll never forget the date, I was
twenty-three and already a flight lieutenant. A torpedo
bomber, that was what they called the plane and that
was its speciality, so the plane and the airman were
given the same name; I was a torpedo bomber. The
Seventy-nine, the aircraft, a real jewel, a wonderful
three-engined Savoia Marchetti, great for taking
anything the antiaircraft guns could throw at her, a
mean-looking machine, one of those that make you
think of corsairs, and we were a bit like pirates ourselves, forced to fight a hit-and-run war by the in-
equality of resources, by the circumstances and by
those thick-skulled idiots who, in the best Italian tradition, sent us into that war in the Mediterranean and
left us to get by on our wits, with no backup either.
A real jewel, I was saying, a wonderful three-engined
job, spotted like some Mediterranean version of a leopard, a hump just above the cockpit for the machine
gunner, one gun facing forward and the other facing
the tail, two tubes peering out of that hump, or 'devil's
hunchback' as somebody nicknamed it; the rudder was
emblazoned with the cross of Savoy and I've lost count
of the number of times we huddled in a rubber dinghy
after ditching in the sea, watching that cross and the
three Fascist symbols in the disks on the upper part
of the wings go down last. The whole lot would finally
sink, Savoy cross, Fascist insignia and all, but it would

remain afloat for hours before this happened. A magnificent machine, a real jewel, there's no other word for it, it gave you goose pimples to pilot her, apart from the machine guns on the lookout in the turret, there was another in the fuselage to fire through the side doors, but the masterpiece, the real warhead, was the thousand-kilo torpedo neatly hidden underneath the belly of the plane. To get down to wave level, to release and place the torpedo in the side of a cruiser was a complicated exercise of instinctive mathematics. You had to come down low on the sea, not to avoid the radar, because we didn't even know the British had such a thing, but to take advantage of the curve of the earth and to make ourselves visible only at the very last moment, six people to each plane: two pilots, one gunner, one radio operator, one photographer—the photos were very important and if you want I'll tell you why—and one engineer. The life expectancy of each torpedo bomber—aircraft and man—was three missions, maybe four, but if you think about the fire power of the battleships, the odds were stacked against your making it back from a fifth mission. That didn't stop us all being proud of being torpedo bombers; we would have been glad to be torpedo bombers for the rest of our lives, but we were all young and innocent. We were still in our twenties, every one of us, as good a group as you would find anywhere, believe me, all united by fear and worries of various kinds, but a great group. The squadron leader was twenty-six, a hero he was; when it seemed he was dead, we took his name and called ourselves the

Buscaglia Group, the most amazing aero-aquatic circus ever seen in the Mediterranean war."

The old man interrupted his flow a moment, stared
at me with his head tilted slightly to one side and then
smiled gently. "Pardon me, I'm assaulting you with
words," he said, "I wouldn't like you to take me for
one of those old folk with an incontinent memory." I
replied, "No, not at all, on the contrary." I was very
interested and was glad to hear what he had to say.
"Fear, that's what it is, fear," he went on, "I have to
talk to you about fear, because if I do, you might be
able to grasp the story more easily. Fear didn't get to
you in the middle of an action, there it was a case of
immediate physical terror, immediately resolved by ca-
tastrophe or luck, the sheer speed of what needed to
be done put you into a kind of trance, it was like
dancing, you had to surrender yourself to an instinctive rhythm, concentrate on the rhythm and not think
of anything else, in any case if a shell caught you full
on, you were dead before you knew about it, you had
to surrender to instinct, to the pure rhythm of the
trajectories which are only crossed by destiny, you
had to connect with that destiny, and dance. Take
Graziani, you know who I mean, Giulio Cesare
Graziani? No, doesn't matter, he's still alive like
me—well, as he was attacking a convoy at Tobruk, in
the act of releasing his torpedo, one hand on the control column and the other on the lever, he noticed
some spots on the windscreen and felt something
damp on his neck, but he was too absorbed by the
vague feeling that after the release there hadn't been

the usual bounce which indicated that the plane was now lighter by a good fifteen hundredweight of torpedo, too busy with the turns, sideslips and climbs which are part and parcel of any getaway, and only when he was out of range of the ships' guns did he put his hand to his neck, and when he pulled it away in horror, he saw that in his palm he held half a human brain, the brain of the photographer in the fuselage, the top of whose head had been blown off by a shell. He turned in terror to his copilot, only to find him slumped over on his side with his shirt covered in blood, behind him the flight engineer was moaning, the gunner, also wounded, came staggering into the cockpit, and announced that the photographer was dead and the torpedo hadn't gone. Everything at the one moment, a moment of some complexity, as they might say today. He made the return journey with a crew of the dead and dying...before darkness fell he happened to notice that on the windscreen, apart from the pieces of human brain, there were also several bullet holes, one of which corresponded to the place at the controls where he normally sat; as it passed by he must have been bent over the release lever, the bullet had torn the epaulette off his flight suit and had gone on to blow off two of the fingers of the flight engineer seated behind. It was night when he landed at Gadurrà. They opened the doors from outside, carried off the dead and wounded, and found him seated at the controls with his hand gripped on the control column, weeping uncontrollably; they had to lift him up bodily and carry him out.

"See what I mean? The fear's not in the action, it

was before and after, when we were standing under
the wing waiting for someone to come running up
with a sheet of paper, or the night before the raid
when we were studying the routes and trying to work
out from the maps what was in store for us. Wrestling
with fear meant pushing back the thought that everything was the last—last shave, last tie knot, last coffee,
last letter, last night in a bed. Buscaglia confessed that
he was often afraid and in a panic over the risk, he
had to fight back those feelings like the rest of us, yet
he was the man in charge. There were some who
simply did not have that feeling of risk, and that
spared them the fatigue of mind and body which the
awareness of danger produces in normal people, but I
sometimes think that the best of them are those who
have that worried look, who are worried and silent;
but there are not really any rules in this matter. Anyway, that's the sort of man Buscaglia was.

"We would set off from Pantelleria or Decimomannu in Sardinia, or from Gerbini at the foot of
Mount Etna, but most commonly from Rhodes in the
Aegean: there the Royal Italian Air Force had constructed a runway with a couple of sheds at one side,
Gadurrà it was called; the takeoff field sloped down
towards the sea, almost as far as the shore, it wasn't
easy to take off with a full cargo in the opposite direction, uphill, when the wind was swirling down
from the hills. Between one sortie and the next, if
there was time, I used to go and sit among the ruins
of Lindos; some evenings the sea, the mountains, the
olives trees and the Doric columns formed a landscape
of such maternal peace that I could hardly believe

there was a war on. War in Trento, where I came from, meant rain, grey skies, winter, frost, but how were you supposed to feel pain, how were you supposed to die, in a countryside like this?

"We took off regularly from Gadurrà to attack convoys of warships and cargo ships; the action would have started well before that, when our agents stationed at Algeciras or Tangiers got a message to Rome warning them of ships entering the Mediterranean through the Straits of Gibraltar. I said it was an operation of high, instinctive mathematics, but it might have been better to say internal mathematics, carried out by a ten-ton aircraft with six people on board, flying at sea level, weaving in and out among ships in a hail of shells and antiaircraft fire. The torpedo had to be released sixty meters above the water at a velocity of three hundred kilometers an hour, while keeping the aircraft on manual and never deviating a centimeter from the horizontal; at the tail of the torpedo there was a little empennage which enabled it to glide, on impact with the water the empennage fell away and the torpedo was transformed from an aerial torpedo into a marine torpedo, so we had something in common with submarines. The point was to place an object over which you had no further control on the surface of the sea: everything depended on the actual firing; afterwards you would as well be sitting twiddling your thumbs. The height and velocity, as well as the tailpiece, were what fixed the torpedo's angle of impact and ensured that it didn't just slide under the waves or bob and bounce like a pebble skimmed over the water by a boy on the beach. In its airborne trajectory, the torpedo maintained the speed of the plane from which it had been launched, three hundred kilometers an hour, but the moment it touched the sea, it fell to seventy, which was why it was important to launch the torpedo as close to the ship as possible; close, but not too close, because the torpedo after entering the water executes a sinusoidal curve before straightening out, and at the lowest point of the curve it could pass at depth under the keel of the ship, fail to make contact and speed away on the far side. Now follow me closely, just pretend you're still at school, or that we're doing a waltz: Considering that from seventy meters of height the aerial trajectory of the torpedo is around three hundred meters, and considering that once it's in the water the torpedo takes another two hundred meters to stabilize at a depth tared on land, and that can vary from two to eight meters depending on the ship you're aiming at, the conclusion is that the minimum distance from which the torpedo can be fired is five hundred meters. In addition, if you fired it from farther off, let's say from one thousand meters, the time it takes for the torpedo to reach even the slowest of vessels would be sufficient to allow the vessel to turn, or get away. A splash in the water beneath an airplane coming up at top speed—they would see the whole thing from the ship and from that moment they had their chance to do their own dance steps, for us it was awesome to see a battleship on the other side of the windscreen, remember we were flying roughly level with the bulwarks, to see it pull around as fast as it could, its prow throwing cascades of water into the air, racing against the time it

would take the torpedo to strike it. That laborious
turn to make leeway was the only chance of escape
the ship had; if at the moment of contact, the torpedo's
angle of impact was too tight or too tangential, the
weapon couldn't detonate—the whole business, the internal mathematics or dance among the cannonades
came down to a straightforward bump, a little knock
or thump between two pieces of iron, just imagine, all
that painstaking precision and all that deadly risk just
for one impact, for one innocuous little collision at sea
between a ship and an ordinary piece of metal, which
then slithers away along the hull and ends up who
knows where.

"If fired from five hundred meters, the torpedo
would take twenty seconds to strike the ship's side,
and if the pilot had calculated correctly the movement
of the target and the angle of impact, the Beta angle,
not even the niftiest of ships had any chance of getting
out of the way. The core of these internal mathematics
was the Beta angle, an angle formed by the direction
of the moving ship and a straight line from the position of the ship to the position of the plane at the
moment of firing. This angle is like a mortgage, or
like a song: I fire taking aim not at where you are but
at where you will be twenty seconds from now if my
calculations are correct. You don't need me to tell you
that some mortgages have to be foreclosed. If the torpedo had twenty seconds to reach its target, after firing
it we, aircraft and crew, had hardly four or five; this
was the most critical phase, the getaway, if getaway is
the right word, sometimes we ended up right on top
of the ship, so there was neither time nor space to

turn, and there was nothing for it but to overfly it so low that we grazed its aerials and turrets, skidding, turning, sideslipping, pulling the plane into sudden inverted climbs, frantically trying all kinds of aerobatic numbers that a triple-engined torpedo aircraft was never built for, but which were marvellous for putting off the antiaircraft gun operators; we could see them swivelling round their machine- and pom-pom guns as we swerved madly overhead.

"It was always hard to get out of a convoy, but after a while it was just as hard to get in. At the beginning, in the first torpedo raids, the British fired on individual aircraft, but then they had a go at the *grand barrage,* which is not a dance step but a wall of flame: as soon as they saw us in the distance they turned the whole of their artillery against us, erecting an impenetrable barrier of shells in the sky, rounded off at sea level by bursts of fire from four- or eight-barrel pompom guns which continually strafed the waves. We had to get through that wall of flame and iron—for us a wall of calculated risk—in perfectly level flying formation, because you needed a horizontal trim and fixed height to drop the torpedo into the sea. When you first entered that sky of black cloud, the airplane started its own dance on the ballistic waves of the explosions, the smoke from the shells made your eyes water, not just the smoke, to tell the truth, and the saliva dried up in your mouth; flying lower than the bulwarks, so low that the spray thrown up by the exploding shells fell on your wings and windscreen, you sneaked into a gap between a destroyer and a cruiser, until you were able to fire the torpedo and make off, zooming up into the skies with one almighty kick on the pedals, leaving the crew to cling onto the struts as best they could.

"In all that murderous chaos, unless there was a loud explosion, nobody could ever say for sure whether or not the torpedo had hit its target; that was why there was always a photographer in the crew, while you and your copilot, eyes streaming, kept your mind on the dance and the mathematics, the photographer, held at the ankles by the gunner, was sticking his head out of the turret on the hump to shoot with his Leica and long-distance lens, taking one photo after another, to get snaps that were used not only to win you a medal, because you couldn't exactly rely on the British to tell the truth about the number of ships that went down or about the damage done to their fleet. Buscaglia wanted the photographs to study the progress of the action, on our side as well as theirs. The moment we touched down, the photographers rushed off to their darkrooms and emerged half an hour later with dripping photographs which ended up on the CO's desk. Fine photos, there's no denying it, an extraordinary, unintended piece of reporting, unforgettable souvenirs for us; at first glance, when you saw that scene again, you couldn't believe you had been in the thick of it, and even less that you'd got out alive. From the photos you were able to evaluate whether the column of water at the side of a ship was just part of the general chaos, or if it was due to the explosion of a torpedo, and how much damage it had caused. You could also work out from the photos the damage to our side, you might see a Seventy-nine engulfed in flames as it went into the sea, and from the type of spray thrown up you could guess if there was any chance of the people on board surviving. There was no shortage of planes ditching in the sea, this was another thing which made us feel like submarines, but everything depended on how you entered the water, on whether or not you were on fire, and whether you were still able to steer. Flaps out, levers down, feet and right arm braced against the instrument panel at the last minute, left hand tugging on the control lever to keep the airplane level as it was swallowed up by waves and spat out again a few seconds later, and if all went according to plan you would feel a violent thud and see water splashing and streaming down the windscreen, and the old Seventy-nine would float. At that point, you got the life raft into the sea, if there was time you grabbed everything useful and destroyed the codes and ciphers, which were bound in lead to make sure they sank as quickly and as deeply as possible.

"I have to tell you that I've ended up in the sea many a time, the first time out of utter stupidity when I was returning from a training flight off Pola. So as to give a wave to some friends on the beach at Sistiana, I came in so low over the sea that the side-engine propellers touched the water, there was a tremendous clang and the tips of the blades bent outwards: I managed to get her to climb a bit but the plane was kept in the air by the central engine alone, and all of a sudden it dropped. The crew dashed into the cockpit, I could feel them staring daggers at me, and sweating buckets though I was, it became a matter of curiosity for them to see how I'd get out of this one, and then a matter of some pride for successfully ditching a plane without anyone having ever shown me what happens to a land plane when it ends up in the water. The second time I ditched, it was in the waters around Pantelleria after sinking my destroyer; you must forgive me if I call it mine, in fact it belonged to a British captain whom I met years later in London, a nice man with a real sense of humor; before we fired the torpedo we had been hit ourselves, then as we flew over the ship we were holed again and I could feel the plane losing power under my feet. Once we were in the sea, as the crew were clambering into the life raft, I perched myself on a wing and set to work with a hammer to detach an aileron for use as a nautical rudder, while the copilot dismantled the compass, something that could always come in handy. We heard them shouting from the life raft and turned just in time to see the destroyer's prow rearing obscenely in the air and the ship sliding under, stern first. This happened in the battle of Mid-June, June '42, I mean. The third time... well the third time I'll leave for the moment.

"In terms of risk, the torpedo bombers were just one step below kamikazes, and presumably that must have occurred to Supreme Command, because in the battle of Mid-August, after the aircraft carrier *Furious* had dispatched about forty Spitfires from a latitude on a level with Algiers to take part in the defense of Malta, an unmanned Seventy-nine, operated by a radio on board a Cant Z sent along with it, took off from Villacidro in Sardinia. The Seventy-nine was packed

with explosives, and was supposed to crash into one
of the biggest ships in the convoy; everything worked
like a dream until they got in sight of the British fleet
off the island of La Galite, here a condenser in the
radio-control mechanism, built in accordance with
the usual penny-pinching philosophy, overheated, the
Seventy-nine failed to respond to instructions, over-
flew the convoy, continued in a straight line towards
Algeria, where it crash-landed. The rescuers were very
puzzled at not finding human remains among the
wreckage. Mid-June, Mid-August—funny names for
battles, names of times not places; however these were
the two great air-sea battles of the Mediterranean, both
fought to prevent the British getting supplies through
to Malta. But for us Malta was already lost, the real
problem was elsewhere. Flying over the front lines,
we had the dubious privilege of seeing before anyone
else that the war was lost. You had only to look at the
sheer number of convoys coming into the Mediterranean, piling up in the ports—and we were supposed
to be hunting them down! We would understand it
all even better later on, during the attacks on ships off
Algiers or Gibraltar, acts of war supposedly, but principally acts of propaganda, phoney raids to fill the
news bulletins and keep up morale, and maybe it did
fool some infantryman in Albania into believing that
the *mare nostrum* was still really ours. We risked our
skins in a state of terror, three or four raids at the
most, remember? We came back from each raid more
and more sure in our minds that it was all going to
end in grief, and this knowledge, believe me, made
everything even more painful and hopeless. One day

in Comiso, they captured an enemy bomber, the crew was British but the aircraft was American; they had mistaken the airfield in Comiso for one in Malta—has anything like that ever happened to you? They glided in to land without a care in the world; the lieutenant on duty realized what had happened and gave orders to hold fire; in fact he made the guard line up to welcome the incoming crew, who stepped out all smiles only to find themselves under arrest. You see, war's got its funny side at times, even if this time it was hardly a laughing matter, because that bomber was the eighth wonder of the world, armed to the nines and with every vital component covered up with thick, solid armor. It was October '42, the war was already over, take my word for it, the Americans landed in Algeria the following month, they landed at one o'clock in the morning of the eighth of November; I remember it well because Buscaglia called us together early that afternoon, quietly said these events were not to upset us, we are at war and you each of you know where your duty lies, we take off in half an hour for Algiers. We were in no condition to attack during daylight hours, because the Spitfires from the aircraft carriers would have massacred us, but we were going to attack in the half-light, as movie people call the light when the sun has just gone down but the sky is still bright, the light we've got just now as you and I are talking, except that then it was well into autumn; we were supposed to arrive over Algiers exactly with that fading light so that we would not be visible to the fighter planes and the ships, but we were supposed to be able to make them out in outline, in the semidarkness that lasts five or six minutes on an autumn afternoon, and there's a fine test of navigational calculation for you, or inner mathematics if you like, one thousand kilometers of distance with twelve planes in formation and a margin of error at the target of a couple of hundred seconds. We took off from Castelvetrano in Sicily, where we had been moved in the meantime, a splendid place for oil, and for wine. Over the Mediterranean we ran into one squall after another, solid columns of rain stretching from the sea to the low banks of cloud overhead; we had to swerve out of their way, changing tack as we went, and obviously at every deviation Buscaglia had to adjust the calculations of time lost, wind drift and bow angle to get us back on course, a beautiful display of navigation by dead reckoning. Finally, in the dark, we caught a glimpse of the outlines of the Atlas Tellien, with the shadows of the great warships over to the west; but we were late, too late, the sun was already down and that was fine, but even the lingering, thin light of dusk was fading second by second, it was five past six on a November evening; Buscaglia gave his orders over the headphones without any trace of emotion—turn back, head for Sicily. Two days later, Buscaglia launched an attack on the Bay of Bougie, to the east of Algiers; along with him he wanted no more than three other planes, commanded by Graziani, Faggioni and Angelucci, who was new to the group, so I stayed at home, not without some disappointment. Instead of attacking from the sea, Buscaglia decided to come at the port of Bougie from the land side, so when they got to La Galite they left the Mediterranean and made for Tunisia, flying very low to the west, turning north to allow them to clear the mountains then swoop down on Bougie harbor. The surprise was less than perfect, because a high-flying German twin-engined plane saw them emerge from inland, took them for British or American and nosedived onto them, at which point everybody opened fire from all sides, there was flak from the ships and the antiaircraft positions on land, the Spitfires took off from the aircraft carriers, Buscaglia and the others bunched together to defend themselves better from the fighters—the bay was a terrifying spectacle for them, they'd never seen so many warships, so many guns and so much firepower. They came down to the usual, harrowing height of seventy or so meters, flying right into round after round of gunfire, they collected a few hits but went straight on. Angelucci and his crew died at that moment, in the barrage the plane was seen bursting into flames, breaking apart and falling into the hills, the corpses were brought back to Italy only a couple of years ago. The others fired off their torpedoes against the cargo ships moored in the harbor, the only target worth bothering about, because warships could be replaced in no time but supplies were still valuable. The problem was that because they were aiming for the docks, they found themselves above the houses and inside the mountainous Gulf of Bougie, they climbed steeply, made a tight turn, grazing the rocks as they did so; at the top of the ascent Faggioni let himself go into a sideslip and lined up under his companions; Buscaglia did likewise, and the whole patrol reversed course and formation, came hurtling down from the heights—a real circus act that must have been! a fine dance step with great, lumbering beasts like those!—and all this in nonstop enemy fire, pure instinct guided by rhythm: those three were the best there were, the most skilled of all the torpedo bombers. They went back across the port, the only escape route open to them; there they were welcomed by more fire from the antiaircraft guns and then, just as they got out of the port, they were picked up by the Spitfires, which fired furiously at them, they huddled together wing to wing once again, at sea level so as to protect their undersides, the most delicate part of the Seventy-nine, and to leave the way clear for their machine gunners, who were firing from the turrets at the pursuing fighters. The Seventy-nine was exceptionally sensitive to the slightest touch: if you had her well in hand you could form a pack by placing your wing between the wing and tail of the next plane. Flying so closely together with such an awkward plane was quite scary the first couple of times; eventually you found the courage, but you still needed perfect engine synchronization, enormous confidence in your patrol leader and an exact level of pressure on the pedal and lever to be able to stay close in without snarling up your companion or having the tip of your wing torn off by the outside propeller. The effect, for anyone pursuing you, was of a solid wall of fire thrown up by the tail gunners, who were limited in their sweep by the need to avoid the rudder and tailplane, so this provided a shadow zone for fighter pilots who had learned to shelter there while riddling you with shots. I have to tell you all this because it will be important in a short while, as you will see, and because it was by flying and firing this way that the three of them were able to get out of the Bay of Bougie, away from a barrage the like of which had never been seen, leaving a few Spitfires groaning in their wake, pierced with bullet holes or else belching smoke as they vanished among the fish.

"When they got back to Castelvetrano, I was there waiting for them near the hangars with the mechanics and all the others, Faggioni appeared at the top of the steps pale and tense; he went over to Buscaglia, who was checking the damage to his own plane, and screamed at him that it was utter madness to attack a well-guarded stronghold like that in daylight, you were just sending men out to die, he said, and to die for nothing. It was surprising to hear that from a man like Faggioni, an extraordinary and highly disciplined pilot, shrewd and responsible enough to know that you don't raise matters like that in front of other officers, NCOs or airmen; but Buscaglia was just as disciplined and exceptional, and for that reason he moved off without saying a word. Graziani took Faggioni to one side to let him vent his rage on him, and anyway these three were the oldest officers, the most responsible in command, and, as you can imagine, it's part of the business of command to know what makes men tick and to pay heed to their feelings. Buscaglia summoned Graziani into his office—'What's going on?' he said. 'I think Faggioni is partly right,' said the other, 'it's crazy to attempt to slip past a whole escort of warships to get at the cargo ships; three out of the four crews got out of Bougie by sheer good luck, purely because the Americans are still feeling their way and shoot at individual targets instead of throwing up a barrage as the British do.' Look," said the elderly gentleman, returning to indirect speech to convey what he could not have heard personally, "Graziani was trying to mediate; there were murmurings in the ranks, the rumor was that Buscaglia was taking too many risks in his pursuit of honors, that he couldn't care less about the men's losses or sacrifices, but this was nonsense and Graziani made light of it: 'You don't need me to tell you,' he said, 'that when we were being pursued by the Spitfires we got away only because all three of us have put in hours of flying in tight formation, wing to wing, but the other officers think that it would be better to drop the torpedoes in the semidarkness of dusk when they can't be seen by the enemy fighters, and I'm basically in agreement with them.' 'I'm not,' said Buscaglia. 'With the rear gunners, if we're flying in tight formation, like today, you can defend yourself more easily from warplanes in daylight, and anyway it's easier to ditch the plane in the sea during the day if you're hit.'" The elderly man came back to the present with the remark, "I wouldn't like you to think that this dispute of daylight versus darkness was a theoretical or academic problem, there was nothing academic about it, any more than there was any theory which was not converted into an immediate, positive, concrete question of life or death. Anyway, Graziani came out of Buscaglia's office without any definite conclusion having been reached over the question of the light.

"That evening we ate in icy silence, in part because

of the day's tension and the comments that had
been passed, in part because of the death of Angelucci
and his crew. Angelucci had a lovely voice, he sang
beautifully, it was left to me to gather together his
guitar, his new, blue Schöller uniform with which he
had probably hoped to make a big impression, his silver cigarette case and a little bundle of letters, and
pack them all up for his family. We all went to bed
early in a big room in the Palazzo Pignatelli in Castelvetrano. Buscaglia had got a hold of a car battery and
lamp. When he noticed that I couldn't get to sleep,
he asked if I was afraid, and I said I was. 'So am
I,' he replied; 'switch on the light and pass me the
map.' He traced out the route with his finger, 'We'll
make our way across Tunisia and Algeria, what do
you think?' 'Good idea,' I replied. During the night
he called to me a few times to check the route again,
after all, I was his aide-de-camp. The following morning we were on the airfield at dawn, ready to go,
waiting for word from Supreme Command. Buscaglia
arrived in his car on the apron; he made Graziani get
in and they drove down to the foot of the runway,
where we saw them get out and walk along a country
road that circled the airfield. There they picked up the
argument about midday light versus nightfall from
where they had left off the previous evening, Buscaglia
with new arguments in favor of daylight. 'The level
of training of some of the officers,' he said, 'does not
provide sufficient guarantee of their ability to return
under cover of darkness, especially with poor weather
or damaged aircraft, so it's better to launch the torpedo attack in early afternoon.' Graziani turned the

argument around to his own advantage, 'if the training level of some of them is so modest, how would
they ever be able to fly in close formation, wing to
wing, and defend themselves from the Spitfires, so
your main argument in favor of daytime rather than
evening flying doesn't stand up.' The elderly gentleman interrupted his narrative. "Of course I know this
might seem to you nothing other than an academic
dialogue on light and darkness held one morning in
the year nineteen hundred and forty-two in a military
airfield in the province of Trapani, possibly under the
influence of the ancient philosophical traditions of the
locality, but I would rather invite you to think of them
as two young men obliged to debate technical and
tactical questions while enclosed inside a shell of their
deepest emotions and convictions. Their discussion, far
from being purely academic, quickly shifted to embrace the whole progress of the war. Graziani fell silent as he became aware of the other's need to find an
outlet for the tension which had overwhelmed him,
and the other released it in a monologue. The war
was moving towards its inevitable conclusion, the enemy forces were much superior, we are being driven
back onto home territory, he said: 'Our group will be
asked to take part in heavy fighting, many of us will
be killed, the more fortunate will end up as prisoners
of war, the few survivors or escapees will be handed
the task of reconstituting the squadron.' Graziani,
fond though he was of Buscaglia, was as sharp as a
needle and tried to propose an alternative, at least a
short-term alternative, to this catastrophic vision. He
began by setting out, in general terms, the case for

inflicting the most serious damage possible on the enemy while keeping our casualties to the minimum; he continued with the observation that crews of our sort were suffering a process of attrition and that new ones could not be trained in a short time span and so, Carlo Emanuele, he concluded, why do we not attack at dusk when the odds are stacked more in our favor? Buscaglia, taken aback by this sudden, renewed assault, abandoned the agonized tone and was reverting to the argumentative style when he was interrupted by the arrival of a motorcyclist from the far side of the airfield with the news that he was wanted on the telephone; shortly afterwards in his office he received an order by telephone directly from the head of Supreme Command, and the order was simplicity itself—back to Bougie, same procedure as yesterday.

"We took off at eleven o'clock in the morning, six warplanes with their respective crews, Buscaglia at the head; as he opened up the throttle, he waved to Graziani who, together with Faggioni, had been grounded since they had both taken part in the previous day's operation. We headed for the open sea, and once we sighted La Galite, came down to sea level and made for Africa; we flew over Tunisia, continued towards Algeria, keeping to the far side of the mountain range which stands guard over the coast, until we were able to bank to the north and enter a valley in the spine of the Atlas Tellien. I have already described that route to you, but it was new to me: we followed the ascent of the valley, the mountainous flanks closing in until they reached a ceiling of cloud; as we climbed, we felt the cliffs pressing in on us, like reservoir walls on river water, and we were squeezed between the ceiling of cloud and the floor of the valley until we soared over the top and went plummeting like a waterfall down from the sky onto the sea and onto Bougie. Obviously, the British were trying desperately to figure out how we'd got there and why no one had picked us up earlier. Buscaglia gave the order over the headphones to get into assault formation, we drew up behind him, my Seventy-nine reached speeds it had never previously approached, everything—controls and bodywork—was shaking, a mad nosedive in a hellish din of metal and wire, not just the whiplash of the cloth on our panels, above us the twenty-millimeter guns of the Spitfires crackled and beneath us the barrels of the naval batteries were spewing out one almighty, violent *grand barrage,* they had mastered it in a single day. The fighter planes made a beeline for Buscaglia, singling out the big prize and ignoring us small fry, his plane burst into flame at the first bursts of gunfire, he went on fearlessly, I can still see in my mind's eye that plane deviating neither to right nor left, dragging a widening trail of smoke in its wake. I was right behind him, I tried to catch up and shelter him, I tried to get in close and fly wing to wing with him but I couldn't reach him, I was already on full throttle, I dropped the nose and that way gained a few feet, but at the cost of losing height; I was out of line and directly underneath him, my machine gunner was firing nonstop but the Spitfires were buzzing frantically on the other side, they got in between us and positioned themselves in the shadow of Buscaglia's plane. They let up only when we came within range of the naval batteries. I was hoping against hope that Buscaglia's crew would manage to control the flames on board, but as we passed over a destroyer the plane received several more strikes and the trail of smoke suddenly expanded. Buscaglia got clear of the ring of escort ships, his plane was blazing furiously but he took aim at a massive liner at anchor and fired off his torpedo. The plane was already low over the sea, it came gliding down and crashed in the bay; when it made contact with the water, it exploded and the burning gasoline spread out over the sea."

The elderly gentleman gave an unexpected sigh which hung in the heavy silence, throwing a furtive glance around him as he did so. "We returned to Castelvetrano in the early afternoon," he said, "arriving one by one. Graziani, who was standing waiting with the mechanics, counted five planes and knew immediately whose was the missing sixth. As we were coming in, Faggioni's plane was returning from Catania and he waited his turn to land. On the ground, passing by our bullet-riddled planes, his photographer and machine gunner made signs to inquire of the mechanics whether anyone was missing, and they indicated with raised forefinger, joined thumb and ring finger the rank of squadron leader. The photographer went along to the cockpit to tell Faggioni, who slammed on the brakes, put his head on the control column and burst into tears.

"Buscaglia was dead. An ace aviator, you will say, and yes, he was certainly that, in spite of the conventions, because ours was not an age of aces; the term belongs to the First World War, a vague definition, indicating exceptional technical and moral qualities, later tightened up by the introduction of precise standards to avoid its abuse; they even went as far as drawing up an official list of First World War aces, a distinction awarded principally to fighter pilots. But we did not shoot down other planes, our targets were ships, and with the passing of the years the concept of fighter pilot underwent a change, it lost its overtones of individual duellist. Our training was all about crews and groups, that was the basic mental, I might almost say emotional, unit, an anti–prima donna spirit enforced by Supreme Command's rigid regulations: they moved us around constantly from one mission to the next to avoid the accumulation of honors; in the dispatches, no matter how sensational the actions were, the principal characters were indicated by their initials followed by rank, so as to discourage swollen egos. And yet, as torpedo bombers we enjoyed a special status, it was spontaneous and involuntary, perhaps because there were so few of us, as was evidenced by the emblem of Buscaglia's squad—four cats lined up on a torpedo, four dumbfounded and perplexed cats under the motto *Pauci sed semper immites;* or perhaps because our line of combat made us amphibian, aero-aquatic, like submariners operating at sea level, or rather taking wing; or perhaps, when all is said and done, it was simply because we were a group. Whatever the reason, the bulletin of the thirteenth November 1942 gave the announcement of the death of our commanding officer with name, surname and decorations awarded for the one hundred thousand tons of shipping he had sent to the bottom of the sea during his various sorties, including the last, and from that day we became the Buscaglia group.

"*Pauci* we were, and becoming fewer by the day, eight officers out of twenty had died in less than eight months; and as for the *immites,* had we the guts to get back into a Seventy-nine, or any other aircraft for that matter, after the death of Buscaglia? And yet, scared as we were, we started flying again: Graziani and Faggioni assumed command, the one of the group, the other of the squadron, but everything became more demanding, the Allied defense was such that we had to cut out daytime and even evening sorties, too many things needed to come together, too many elements all constantly shifting—us, the convoys sailing the Mediterranean, the sun in its brief, twilight span. Night and night attack was all we had: darkness saved us from the Spitfires but tied us to the moon and its phases, we began to think in terms of waning and crescent moons as though we were Red Indians; at full moon we could make out the surface of the sea, attacking into the moon we could make a guess at the ships' silhouettes, but even so, often you couldn't see as far as your nose. One night in the bay of Philippe-ville pulling out of a dive I glanced at the altimeter: it stood at ten meters below sea level. I pulled back the throttle with all my might and shut my eyes, the altimeter was still calibrated to Castelvetrano pressure, which was different from that of the Algerian coast, but how great was the difference in meters, in centi-meters? How close had I come to the surface of the water without seeing a thing? With night flying we became familiar with the unsettling effects of the

searchlight, beams of light which shone on the windscreen, then veered off to the side at the last moment;
it was a new and alarming optical effect, disembodied
blows which it became instinctive to ward off by making the plane yaw one way then another, or by air-
braking and diving desperately. We flew with lights
out, in constant fear of the wings touching, but out of
nowhere, from land or sea, on would go the search-
lights: the first time it was like a cannonade of blinding light, I couldn't see the phosphorescence of the
instruments, nor could I make out what was going on,
and for a few seconds I completely lost control of the
plane. The Seventy-nine had blinds over the wide side
windows and over the big windows above the windscreen, and for a while we flew with blinds down.
Soon afterwards the Spitfires adopted the tactic of
waiting for us above the airfield as we returned from
our mission: we would get back in the dark totally
worn out, sometimes with a damaged plane or with
wounded men on board; they would make out the
reverberations of the engine exhaust, or see the rocket
we fired to alert ground crew to switch on the runway
lights, and at that point they would open fire and
come chasing after us, forcing us to race off, scared
witless, at the level of the fields and up over the hills,
in total darkness.

"One night in January '43 my turn came, my number came up, one night with no moon, not that you
could rely on her for a good turn if you were going
into combat. We took off at eight in the evening from
Decimomannu in Sardinia for the Bay of Bona in
Algeria, we fired our torpedo against a ship in the

most perfect darkness, when all of a sudden the sky was lit up with a firework display of piercing beams and machine-gun fire. Outside the bay we found the usual fighters lying in wait, but we shook them off by swooping down to sea level. We had been holed in several places but without any too serious damage, so we stayed low and headed back to Sardinia. All of a sudden, an hour into our flight home, there erupted from the darkness beneath us a geyser of shells and dazzling jets of light; the night was so dark and the sea so black that we had been overflying a convoy without even being aware of it. We were hit in various places and just when it seemed we were going to get a ay with it, all three engines suddenly broke down. At that altitude, there was no chance of keeping airborne and no time to think: we sent an uncoded SOS; I got ready to ditch for what was the umpteenth time, but the first when I couldn't see a thing, neither the horizon nor the sea line. I stared at the instruments on the flight deck, the anemometer and altimeter, and waited. We entered the water at two hundred an hour, one almighty crash into a gluey wall, the power of the deceleration hurtled us all forward, I banged my head against the bombsight with its handles and racks. When the plane bobbed back up onto the surface, my thumb was pulp and one eye was oozing blood. I raised my good hand, groped for the door above the pilot's seat, got it open and crawled out into the biting wind and driving rain, and if I'd been emerging from a submarine at sea in the middle of the night, it couldn't have been worse; I leaped onto one of the wings and it was like plunging into a frozen well of utter darkness. Someone got a life raft into the water, we managed to get in, each one of us wounded some-where, and the Seventy-nine floated off with its nose under water and its tail in the air. We drifted, numb with cold, sprays of salt water burning our wounds, but at least they kept us awake. We had no way of knowing we were only fifteen miles off Capo Sparti-vento, nor that the signal station on the island of Sant'Antioco had seen us go down and given the alarm, although we only learned the worst at day-break, when an auxiliary vessel picked us up: we had ditched in a mined area, so to rescue us they had to clear the whole zone, then lay down the mines again.

"I woke up in hospital swathed in bandages, I had come out of it the worst, but I'm a fast healer and some weeks later they took off the dressings and let me out of bed. But in the following days, as I wan-dered around the corridors, I seemed to be constantly bumping my shoulder into the walls or into the door-ways, as though I had lost that instinctive balance we all have when we walk. I mentioned this to the doctor and was immediately sent back to bed with the strict order to stay absolutely still. They gave me a weird pair of glasses with only one tiny hole to see through, and a couple of weeks later they announced that when I banged my head and eye against the bombsight, a film had formed over the retina and closed it up, but maybe, just maybe, with treatment it would reopen. San Remo, where I spent the spring, was beautiful, one huge convalescent center for the wounded of all the services. In the evening I would go for a stroll along the promenade; I knew only too well that I would never be going back to the group, for me the war was over, but staring at the sea from the shore gave me an odd feeling of solidity and protection. The Riviera was magnificent, I was one of Fortune's favored and yet I felt a nostalgia for the old times, at any moment of the day I knew exactly what the others were up to, it took no effort to picture it in my mind's eye, especially on my evening strolls when I stopped to gaze at the moon, which was no longer for me a source of the light you needed for survival but had reverted to being a poignant, metaphysical embellishment of night's landscape.

"Out of the blue in autumn I received two letters, one from Graziani and the other from Faggioni. The armistice had taken Graziani by surprise while he was on leave in Rimini, and he had wasted two days talking to the Germans and contacting Rome for orders; finally, under a hail of bullets from an Italian artillery squadron, he stole a Seventy-nine from the airfield at Fano and landed in Catania. As he was taxying along the runway, he was met by a jeep driven by a smiling American soldier, a lieutenant who spoke perfect Sicilian; on the ramp, he shook hands enthusiastically with each member of the crew, offered them cigarettes, then produced a cine camera from the jeep and asked them to get back inside and make their appearance at the door one more time while he shot his film. Graziani had to repeat the scene several times, the final time for the Catania airport commander, a colonel of the United States Air Force. There was enormous excitement among the Americans when they discovered it was a torpedo bomber: they stuck under his nose a wad of photographs taken from various ships during torpedo attacks; among the planes racing about like cats in heat Graziani picked out his own more than once, and it was only then he realized that certain ships really had been sunk. Then the Intelligence Service put to him various detailed questions about the system of air defense in Italy, matters about which he had no knowledge. The Americans didn't believe him, and were not persuaded by the fact that he had headed south immediately and of his own accord, they put him in charge of a group of Seventy-nines transporting mail and officers between the mainland and the islands, and for some months he had a military policeman sitting at his back, whose job was to file a report every evening on every single thing he had done during the day.

"Faggioni too was on leave on the day of the armistice, and he too stole a Seventy-nine, from Florence-Peretola airport, and along with it he stole the mechanic he had asked to check it over. He landed at Littoria, where the rest of the unit was. Desperate times, believe me, appalling times, almost impossible to obtain orders, difficult to grasp what was going on or to make decisions, the Germans were closing in on the airports, the following morning Faggioni and the rest loaded men, munitions and spare parts onto thirteen planes and took off for Ampugnano airfield, Siena, the only free base after the fall of Pisa and Littoria. In Siena, in the general turmoil and complete breakdown of communications, they received first an order to make their planes unusable by removing the air-intake ducts from the engines, an order they declined to carry out, then an order to proceed to Milis in Sardinia, an airport which some said was already occupied by the Germans. They took off at dawn and the moment they were over the Tyrrhenian it was clear, there in the sky, what each one had concluded about the armistice, the choice was tacitly declared by a swift turn and change of course. They separated over the sea without a word, one Seventy-nine heading north, another four making for Sicily, and only one landing on the mined runway at Milis, where the crew was immediately taken into custody by the Germans; the others, watching the scene from above, headed south. Faggioni, travelling separately with a group of four planes, flew without any difficulties as far as Bocche di Bonifacio, then one of his planes was attacked by a Messerschmitt 109 and forced to ditch, another was buzzed by two Focke Wulf 190s and forced down into the sea off Capo Testa; Faggioni saw some Seventy-nines parked around the airfield at Milis but no sign of the green rocket giving them the all-clear for landing. He attempted to land at Borore, but was dissuaded by two red rockets followed by two shells. He turned back and, keeping in formation with the other plane, returned to Ampugnano as per last orders received. For three days they lived on the deserted airstrip as though they were in some godforsaken outpost, until one day a civilian on a bicycle, who turned out to be the ex-commander of the base, arrived with the evacuation order. They applied to the headquarters at Siena for clarification, and both were given one month's leave. Faggioni's lasted four days, at the end of which he presented himself at the

Training Academy of the Regia Aeronautica at Cascine air base and enlisted for a body which did not yet exist, but which was to become the aviation corps of the Italian Social Republic. He died at midnight on Easter Monday 1944, while torpedoing American ships anchored off Anzio under the April new moon: he always said it's hard but as long as I'm able I'll go on; he called cargo ships 'big bellies,' and perhaps even in that last attack he issued the order over the headphones—Let the big bellies have it!—a funny war cry to be sure, and we always used to laugh at him about it. They fished his beret and briefcase out of the sea near Anzio.

"Anzio is not too far from Naples," the elderly gentleman began again, "and not far from Naples itself stands the town of Ottaviano Vesuvio, and not far from there was Campo Vesuvio, an airstrip set up by the Americans; among the vines flanking the runway, a bomber flight of the Regia Aeronautica was bivouacked. Graziani instructed pilots on the Baltimore, a two-engine aircraft supplied by the new allies for pilot training, spending his days in dual-control flight with his pupils, and one afternoon in July, while engaged in lessons around the airfield, he saw a Seventy-nine in service as a passenger transport come in to land; nothing unusual about that, the plane often carried high-ranking officers, but what was strange was that the control tower invited him to land as well. Taxying up to the parking area, he passed near to the newly landed plane, and one figure in a bright new uniform detached himself from the group of officers around the ramp and came over to him. Do you know who it was?" asked the elderly gentleman. "No, you can't know, you could never imagine, nobody could have imagined, not even Graziani himself until he found himself face to face with the other man. It was Buscaglia. Carlo Emanuele Buscaglia in flesh and blood. Risen from the dead. Graziani stared at him without speaking a word, they embraced, Buscaglia said to him with tears in his eyes, 'You're still in the thick of things.' The last time they had spoken to each other was before takeoff for Bougie, the morning of the argument over the light, a year and a half previously at the airfield in Castelvetrano in Sicily. Buscaglia had to depart at once for Lecce, there was some minister shouting from inside the airplane, but he said he would be coming back the following month to take command of a bomber unit and then they would have time to talk. True to his word, he returned the following month to do a training stint on the Baltimore, and one August night at the foot of Vesuvius, sitting in front of the tent that was their quarters, Buscaglia told Graziani his story. The Americans had picked him up in the Bay of Bougie, picked him up and stitched him together, then dispatched him to a POW camp in Texas. The only thing he remembered about the crash landing was the slow agony of the plane's photographer, the only one apart from himself to have survived in that sea of blazing oil; as he died he cursed Buscaglia for having run those excessive risks, and that memory made Buscaglia burst into tears. But his story started further back, at the time when, even before Castelvetrano, he had given orders for his plane to be placed under police guard day and night, an order no one could understand at the time but which was the result, he now explained, of confidential advice from the Bishop of Catania to keep the planes, and most especially his own, under strict surveillance, since he had heard talk about possible sabotage in the unit. And in fact, said Buscaglia, someone must have interfered with the equipment, because at Bougie, under fire from the Spitfires, the guns on his Seventy-nine had jammed on the first round because of defective cartridges. He obtained proof of sabotage on his return to Italy, when many political and military authorities sought him out, even Palmiro Togliatti invited him along to the Naples headquarters of the Communist Party. Togliatti praised him to the heavens for backing the Constitution, but also reproached him for having sounded off about victory two years previously when replying to a speech by some Fascist dignitary from Catania on an official visit to the group. Togliatti had informed Buscaglia that there was a Communist cell already operating at that time among the torpedo-bomber personnel, and Buscaglia instantly attributed to them responsibility for the sabotage of the ammunition. He was surprised that only the Church and the Communists seemed in possession of worthwhile information, but he remained convinced that if the weapons had worked he would not have ended up the sea. In the same way, responsibility for the malfunctioning of the torpedoes which, to the equal amazement of those who launched the strikes and those who were struck, did not explode on impact, was to be laid at the door of the powerful Communist cell operating in the torpedo-manufacturing plant at Maiano near

Naples. The night was hot and humid there at the feet of Vesuvius; Buscaglia told Graziani how he was the object of reverential deference among Italian prisoners of war on his entry into the Monticello POW camp but of general contempt on exit because of his decision to side with Badoglio. But the decision was the right one, he continued, and in keeping with his duty as a soldier, it gave him the opportunity to put himself once again at the service of his country, in the work of national reconstruction, and for that reason he had requested and obtained a command. At the foot of the volcano the night was long and hot, the moon was ringed by humid vapors; Buscaglia reminisced and speculated, slipping effortlessly from the past to the present and from the present to the future: he would complete his training on the Baltimore as soon as possible, would get back into action, he had plans which stretched far beyond the liberation of Italy, once the war in Europe was won he expected to take up a position in the Allied armed forces with a command of his own, he would go to the Pacific, would transform the Baltimores from simple bombers to torpedo bombers, would take up the old fight, with Japanese shipping as the final objective.

"In the days following, he heeded the advice of Graziani, who took him up with him on training flights and remarked that the two years of inactivity had made him rusty; he recommended that, since the crucial controls of American planes differed considerably from Italian ones, he do a spot of ground practice with a Baltimore, no more than taxying along the runway, and this Buscaglia did with great humility and application. Then one evening when, even though it was still light, the airfield had closed down for the night and the officers were already at dinner, a lieutenant presented himself at the officers' mess to tell the base commander that Squadron Leader Buscaglia would like him to go and witness his takeoff. Since it had been agreed that each pilot prior to solo takeoff was required to carry out a stated number of dual-control flights, which were Graziani's responsibility, the base commander turned to the wing commander, who turned to Graziani, who replied without hesitation that it would be better if the squadron leader undertook further sessions. The lieutenant was ordered to report this to the squadron leader, and he went off to do so. In the distance, the rumble of engines being started up could be heard, but no one paid much heed; often the mechanics worked overtime, especially in the long, light evenings of late August. Then there was the unmistakable roar of engines at full throttle. Then a sudden, dreadful silence. Graziani dashed out of the mess, the others after him; the mechanics were already running at full pelt across the vineyards in the direction of a black cloud on the far side of the airfield. The lieutenant said that he had relayed the order to Buscaglia, who was already seated in the Baltimore with the engines racing, that he had clambered up onto a wing to tell him not to fly. Buscaglia had thought it over for a few seconds, then said, 'Pull down the hatch, I'm going to have a go, I'm taking off.' He had taxied up to the beginning of the runway, opened up the engines, raced down three hundred meters on full power until the wheels lifted slightly off the ground, the plane seemed suspended in midair, pitched on its nose, slewed over on one wing, which broke off, causing the gasoline to ignite. Buscaglia had had the strength to climb out of the cockpit, he even got free of the enveloping flames, then collapsed to the ground, unconscious. In the infirmary, the medical officer immediately informed Graziani of the seriousness of the situation, and later, when Graziani was admitted to the room, Buscaglia looked at him from between his bandages and broke down; he wept, prayed to God, begged to be helped to recover again. He was transferred to the British hospital in Naples, but during the night his condition deteriorated and he died at dawn."

The elderly gentleman fell silent, swept his hand over the table, the movement causing his elegant tie pin to sparkle in the reflected moonlight. Neither he nor I would have been able to say precisely how that light had changed; evening had fallen on the airfield with slow, catlike steps, obscuring little by little the horizon and our faces. "I hope I haven't bored you with all this chatter," he said, and I replied, "Not in the slightest." "You see," he added, "I still fly, I'll continue flying until the medics tell me to stop, and I'm over seventy already, I fly in the same planes as you, but I'm never going to forget that big three-engined, turreted beast with leopard spots. Isn't it funny, it must be a feeling peculiar to this century, I doubt if anybody experienced it before. In that metal belly, I knew terror, I felt pain in every part of my body, I saw people I loved die, it was my youth, months like years, years like decades, everything so intense, so unreal. I still fly and when the sky has a thick ceiling of cloud, I burst through it and soar away, it's a different world above the clouds, it's like squatting in the attic, peering down at your house; the sky above the clouds is a magnetic memory, everything is still imprinted on it, as though on the silver salt paper they use in photographs, and anyway where would be the sense if everything that once existed had just disappeared for good, don't you think? I can't bring myself to believe that above the clouds, in the headquarters of all that has occurred at least once, I won't some day be aware of a shadow drawing up close to me, a paunchy, resolute shadow, a shadow with a duty to perform, and that duty is the iron cylinder sticking out from its underbelly; you can tell they are hard at work in that shadow, you can tell from the machine gunner in the upper section, back turned to the nose and attention fixed on the tailplane, you can tell from the blinds drawn over the windows in the cockpit. I would turn on the radio and call them, using the number painted on the fuselage, they wouldn't reply, perhaps on account of the radio silence imposed when on a mission, or perhaps because I have already made it home from my mission while theirs is still under way, just look at how intent, serious and concentrated they all are. I would draw up wing to wing, and it might even seem to me that they have slowed down just to make it easy for me to do so, I would make a sign to the gunner but he, with no show of fear, wouldn't turn his head, how could he miss me? I would switch on the radio and call them again, using their names this time, and since the blinds prevent me from seeing who is in charge, I would use all the names they might reply to, names which come back to me one by one, and then gently from the silence of my loudspeaker I would hear a crackle, a syllable, a word, but so low, so distant that it would be impossible to make anything out, I would be so pleased to have established contact, so overcome with emotion that I would yell into the microphone, 'Repeat! Repeat!' and do you know what would come down the radio waves? Do you have any idea, my dear sir, what would emerge from my onboard radio? It would be a crooning voice, an old Italian swing number, and I'd recognize the voice, I know that voice, I would say, of course I do, it's the singer Di Palma, don't you hear him...what a voice!

> ...I've got a date with the moon tonight,
> Just out of town when the sun goes down,
> I'm glad that she's no lady
> And for sure she'll not be late.
> So forget the film, and forget the show,
> And you won't see me at the bar,
> You're on your own tonight, my love,
> And let me tell you why.
> 'Cause I've got a date with the moon tonight,
> At nine o'clock in a shady spot
> Bee bibbity baw, bee bibbity bow
> Ba ba, beebbity bow..."

Reaching Dew Point

ONE MORNING, WHILE airborne, you lost your way, as people do in life, without ever being quite aware that they are lost but drifting bit by bit into a zone where their bearings are gone: first the countryside was not what you expected, then the river which ought to have come into view did not, and finally the heat haze which hung over the Po valley crystallized into a more unyielding, impenetrable opaqueness. Any minute now I'll be out of this, you thought, and the minute passed, then another, one by one the windows of the plane turned frosty white and you came to realize that there was no way out of that hot, daytime mist. It is not the case that people lose their way in an instant, the process will be under way over time, you had, in reality, already got lost earlier, at the last checkpoint, when you called Air Traffic Control confirming your position as the spot where you ought to have been as per flight plan; pure nominalism, the victory of the plan over reality, since you were nowhere near there. At that point, you made a descent to a lower altitude, following closely a railway track, but when the line came to a halt in a little village, you were reduced to flying low over the village station in an effort to make out its name, but the name, glimpsed as you flashed by at speed, was of no great help; wherever you were, you were lost and climbing once more into the haze; you lost your bearings more comprehensively until you found yourself where you are now, which is to say, you have no idea where. The last sure position was Abeam Boa, a nautical point on the map a dozen or so miles to the east of Bologna, above various tiny huddles of houses—Budrio, Medicina or San Lazzaro di Savena, who could say?—the one indistinguishable from the other; the village name not being written on the house roofs; no one ever heeded Rodchenko when he proposed that the roof become a heaven-facing façade which would offer aviators something more than the monotony of rows of tiles. This occurred in the thirties, but the roof-façade never caught on after that; roofs have remained uniform, as uniform as the villages which do not carry names on their roofs, and as a result you were lost, and lied about your fix to Air Traffic Control.

Fear is composed of liquids in the act of drying up: you stared at the altimeter, you grabbed at the map, searching wildly for those dark-colored areas in shades ranging from warm yellow to dark brown, where the mountain peaks are clustered; if you were off course to the northeast, Monte Venda should be there, if to the north, the Lessini mountains and the Pre-Alps should make an appearance; but you would hardly have time to see a cliff face emerge from the whiteness in front of the windscreen. It was the first time you had got lost in a plane and, not having yet acquired expertise in instrument flight, you celebrated the event with a phrase produced spontaneously by the mind; the phrase ran, "I do not want to die," a phrase which came so naturally that of its own accord your voice spoke it aloud, as though it were the voice of another person reproaching you for exposing him to such a situation. In order to cheat death I must climb, you immediately thought, it is senseless to plough blindly forward. And climb I do, in spirals around the vertical axis of my present position; if I manage to hold perfectly the center of the rotation, if I do not waver on the first or second loop, I am safe. You read on the map the heights of the most likely peaks, adding another thousand feet for safety, and started to climb towards the five thousand mark. In the opaque darkness of the sky, in the infinity of space, slowly drifting upwards in fibrous mist, you closed yourself inside the safety cylinder of your circling flight. All around, everything prickled with invisible menace; with each circle you reduced the radius to reduce the threat, or that was your hope, but each circle was never-ending. Fog is infertile cloud, so Aristotle held, place no trust in that all-permeating, all-enveloping substance, water of that sort is only humidity, not impregnating rain, which sows life in the fields and swells the course of the rivers. Fog is a backdrop, fog lurks; on fields, in the space between earth and sky, fog is sterile, the trusty crony of crime. Unconscious crimes, indifferent to the fog, but crimes nonetheless.

Such were the thoughts in your mind as you kept

an eye on the instruments, variometer five-hundred-feet climb-rating, sixty knots for the steep ascent, turn-and-slip indicator with ball centered and needle tilted for two-minute turn. And yet when you are not flying, you are fond of fog, when a fog descends on the city, you respond first to its scents and changing noise patterns, you feel yourself irresistibly drawn by the night and the mists, like a dog called to heel by its master's whistle. That apart, what did you know about fog, pilot?—that it is born of a coincidence, a coincidence of dew temperature and air temperature, temperatures which you studiously avoided asking the meteorological office to check before takeoff. You could, of course, do so now, you could ask the Air Traffic Control Board if they had any information on the mist, on how widespread it was, on what height it reached, but then you would have to clarify other matters with the Board, so you put it off. Board: philosophically, a concept not amenable to definition, but merely to clarification; Board, one and indivisible but distinct from all others; Board, intelligible and lovable in and of itself alone. Even the Air Traffic Control Board could be understood in these terms; in the last analysis it is the disembodied voice grasped in the mist, the unseen voice speaking from earth, the reversal of the higher and lower orders, with us poor mortals wandering lost in the skies and the Immortal at peace on earth, a pursuing eye in the dark inside the luminous dial of the radar tracers. Eye for eye, Board for Board, there is nothing to be seen here, you caught yourself muttering nervously to yourself; the mind was protecting itself from terror by generating a brand of

nonsense which resembled the "white vision," that
gentle flooding of light which those who pass through
death but make their return claim to have witnessed
at the last moments, the ultimate analgesic with which
the mind gives you its final embrace even as it extin-
guishes itself and prepares to depart.

Outside the windows, the fog seemed to come to
life in thick, darting, smoky forms. It took you some
time to realize that these were not crags, trees or bodies looming out of the darkness, about to collide with
you, but swirls and empty volumes of the humid mass;
you leaned over towards the instrument panel, you
looked upwards in the futile hope that the light of the
sun might dilute that glutinous brightness, but instead,
as you climbed, the opaqueness, growing ever darker,
turned a gloomier grey. The pitching and rolling of
the plane increased, there were sudden updrafts and
downdrafts and a yawing from side to side, swinging
the aircraft around without allowing it to bank, sending it into a flat roll around an imaginary vertical pivot
bored through from the top, as though it were a fish
on a skewer. You rammed down your foot the moment you heard the propeller roaring as it bit into the
air at a different tempo, you rammed down your foot
to regain balance. Had you any idea where you were?
Clear of the fog, certainly, but not in the open sky;
you had gone directly from fog to cloud without as
much as glimpsing a patch of blue, and there you were
in the heart of a cloud, a cumulus to judge by the
turbulence shaking the plane and by the dark surroundings, as livid grey as a bruise. And just how
much did you know then about a *cumulonimbus,*

pilot?—that it held everything inside it, strong rising and falling air currents, rain and hail, the prospect of instant ice; that a cloud of this sort is produced when the air freezes to dew point, and the idea of dew as a thermic reference point, the idea that dew was related to events of might and menace so much greater than itself, dew which has always been consolation, relief, comfort? . . . well, it was not easy to credit. In summer, you had been able to fly around a storm because you had seen it in good time; some miles off you had made out this congested, cylindrical squall stretching from earth to sky, as humid and opaque as a jellyfish, sometimes so precise and fixed in mass that it is possible to circumnavigate it, flank it with one wing, keeping it to the east, since virtually everything in our skies moves from west to east. But this time you had blundered into cloud without knowing where it came from, and not imagining where that sky might end.

The aircraft was buffeted by gusts of wind from below, which raised it onto its side only to let it fall with a dull thud against fresh layers of rising air, as though it were dropping into the furrow of a wave so hollow that the sea itself seemed to have run dry. You had instinctively reduced velocity when you felt the plane twist and turn, you had already lost all sense of direction long before, and after all those climbing turns and that turbulence you had less idea of bearing than ever; you could no longer delay making contact with Air Traffic Control. Hand on microphone, gaze fixed on the blackness of the sky, you worked out what to say. In reality, the words had already shaped themselves in your mind into one natural, grand sentence: "Treviso radar, I do not want to die. I repeat, I do not want to die." Aeronautical jargon, however, leaves no space for wishes, not even for heartfelt wishes, only for positions and directions, although this might well turn out to be an advantage, considering that the terror of being lost in the midst of those clouds was now more or less equal to the fear of having to admit as much to Air Traffic Control. To discover where you are, or to be located again from the ground, all you have to do is own up to your present, miserable condition without wasting a second searching for the aeronautically most accurate, and least humiliating, formula. Call Air Traffic Control, call at once; while you dither, things at this end are getting out of hand, any time now you will fall prey to those illusory sensations which until now you have only read about in the handbooks you flick through last thing at night, before dropping off. You refuse to give in, you simply refuse to face the fact that you are lost, you are still putting the final touches to the words, you fail to notice that the plane is falling on one side, until finally you switch on and declaim in the most impersonal, flat tone you can manage: "Treviso radar, India Echo November is no longer in Victor Mike Charlie. Request a Quebec Delta Mike."

If your aim was to take cover behind a wall of words, you have carried it off. Treviso radar is the authority you are calling, a military authority as it happens; India Echo November is the abbreviated name of this poor machine lost in the skies; Victor Mike Charlie, VMC, are the initials for *Visual Meteorological Conditions*, so you are no longer flying in meteorological conditions of visibility. They might believe that you were not to blame for ending up in fog and cloud, that the state of the sky, the cosmos around you, just happened to alter, that visibility was snuffed out, that previously excellent conditions faded as inexplicably and suddenly as lights fail in a house. (Away from flight and the present situation, in the domain of *everything else*, you would have detested such a use of words as a way of hiding behind "objectivity" and "putting on a brave front"; for years you had heard people speak in this style, using words as though they were precious stones. Through objectivity, that is through omissions, they managed to attribute to things a plausibility they could never possess, making them appear the opposite of what they really were.) *The Quebec Delta Mike*, QDM, you requested is a dated term of the old Q code, the code used by Faggione and Buscaglia. Nothing in the world is more conservative than aeronautical and maritime jargon, QDM, qudimike, an old term much loved by pilots, a term redolent of home comforts, but it is untranslatable because these are not initials but three letters which codify and seal the following, lifesaving question: Be kind enough to inform me of the direction I must follow if I am to reach my destination, *destino* in Spanish, the only language in which the geographical goal coincides with the completion of the individual, personal adventure.

"India Echo November. Position?" replied the voice at the other end. Air Traffic Control's voice was Neapolitan, military and impassive, seemingly emerging from nowhere.

He's got you there. Now what can you say? Where are you? Once more you attempted to play for time, the aircraft tossed about, the sky grew darker by the minute, the voice repeated with a touch of alarm: "India Echo November. Are you receiving? Over."

"Affirmative . . . Four-fifths . . . India Echo November has left Abeam . . ." This much was true, you had left Abeam Boa, but when, how much time previously, and for where? In addition, you were supposed to declare your new altitude. "Levelled at five thousand."

"What do you mean at five thousand?" Neapolitan Air Traffic Control came back immediately, shaken rudely awake. "You're at five thousand? You should have told us if you were going up to five thousand. It's your responsibility to inform us of any change of altitude . . . Do you have a transponder?"

"Yes, we have a transponder." Of course you had the automatic reply mechanism to radar signals, but the royal plural had a merely grotesque, hypocritical and pretentious ring in your present solitude; all those "Do you all have? We have," 's were designed to give the impression of a full crew, the copilot busying himself with inserting the four-figured code the moment it was transmitted, the engineer keeping his eye on the levels, the navigator in charge of the route, the radio operator overseeing communications with the world at large.

"Squawk ident six four six seven," Air Traffic Control insisted.

"Ident six four six seven." You insert the four figures into the instrument, you observe the panel light

flickering, a sign that the radar equipment is inter-
rogating the metallic mass in the sky perceptible to it
alone, but holding you inside it: the transponder replies, and on the ground, in the luminous dial which
records the traces, the indeterminate point which corresponded to your plane lights up with the number
6467: no longer indefinite, you are now distinct,
individualized, singular and knowable.

"Sorry about the altitude," you proceed in the plural, "we've left Victor Mike Charlie. We'd be glad of
a Quebec Delta Mike for the Chioggia VOR," indicating that you always think it's better to climb to a
safe height before making radio contact.

"The qudimike's one zero three," concedes the
Neapolitan voice, in a businesslike tone.

One hundred and three. You began a one-hundred-
and-three-degree turn, heading southeast, a turn in the
clouds in the midst of nonstop bumpiness and updrafts; Air Traffic Control could see where you were
and where the VOR was, relativity of positions, in-
evitability of positions, as in the classical conundrum
on free will—two people, each unaware of the other,
are heading for the same street corner, a third party
at a window sees them approach and foresees the
collision but can do nothing to prevent it; destiny is
foresight minus the power of intervention. At that moment of your life, destiny was a one-hundred-and-
three-degree rotation, and on that figure on the face
of the gyroscopic compass, pulling out of the turn, you
halted, or rather, in the general shambles, attempted
to halt, the body of the plane.

It was then, looking at the artificial horizon, that

you realized the plane was rolling to one side and had almost overturned. You drummed one finger on the instrument, it must be out of order, you felt the plane to be perfectly horizontal and level after the completion of the turn; you peered through the windscreen for confirmation, but everything outside was grey and opaque, giving no fixed point for checking; turning back to the instrument panel, you became aware that the ascent ratings given by the variometer were extremely high while velocity was falling. You could not make out what was happening to the plane, you still seemed to be maintaining perfectly level flight, but was it possible for the entire instrument panel to have broken down all at once? You wondered if, as you travelled through the clouds, ice had formed on the instruments' external air ducts, but you could not remember the means by which each instrument, once it stops receiving the air it requires, indicates position. A pilot in an emergency situation can only make effective use of five percent of what he knows, says Bruno, and if he knows very little at the best of times, what will he be like when the odds are against him? That's why, every night, before going to sleep, you used to read the handbooks leading to further qualifications, and from one of the pages on instrument flight, flicked through when you were half asleep and the book about to drop from your hand, you managed to regurgitate the notion of illusory sensation. Such sensations had to do with the perception of space, they were a function of the fluids in the canals of the auricular labyrinth, whose flow is determined by a movement which causes them to stimulate the cilia in the ear walls and alert us to our own position. So, pilot, you carry flight instruments inside your ears, except that your instruments are a little slower; those dense bodily fluids move more slowly than does the turning aircraft, the cilia in the labyrinth take note and transmit, all in order but all delayed, and so produce a false present in the mind while the aircraft, and your body, are already living in the future, in a different position. You are not at all straight and level, as you believed, and as a true horizon would confirm to you; sight being preeminent, a visible line between heaven and earth would override any other representation of things, and then you would realize, if the clouds were ever again to open, the position you really are in— sitting over to one side inside a plane tilted over on one wing, nose pointing upwards. Be a believer in instruments, Bruno used to say with that ironic imperative he loved to use, if you can't see out, never raise your eyes from the panel, place your trust in instruments alone, and you indeed began to believe and trust blindly, peering at dial hands and figures, constantly tugging at levers, working at pedals and columns until the control column, after a bout of odd vibrations, all of a sudden went limp and weak in your hands, and you knew exactly what was wrong, oh yes, this time you had no doubts: this was a stall, you were going into stall. I do not want to die, your voice rang out loud and clear, I cannot die here, it would clash with my survivor's nature, and while you were speaking or thinking or yelling these words, the aircraft plummeted, tumbling over on its side.

It is hard to say how you fell, or which was the right and which the wrong way up, and for that reason, or perhaps on account of hearing the Neapolitan ask on your radio, "India Echo November, any problems?"—this on seeing you on the radar screen lose a thousand feet in three seconds—whatever the reason, as you fell with no above and no below, your mind filled with images of Cola Fish, the water child so dedicated to the waters of the sea that his own mother cursed him, "May you turn into a fish," and from that day he lived as a fish, or as near to being a fish as may be, submerged in the water for hours on end as though in his natural element, with no need to rise to the surface for air. In order to travel, he permitted himself to be swallowed by one of the giant fish with whom he was acquainted, and he journeyed in its belly just as you were journeying towards the abyss in the damp belly of the great cloud; once he had arrived at his destination, he slit open the fish's stomach with his knife, and emerged into the water to carry out his inquiries as the King's agent. The King was curious to know about the sea bed and Niccolò, after an investigative sojourn in the deep, returned to report that it consisted of coral gardens scattered with precious stones, and with piles of treasure, weapons, human skeletons and bric-à-brac from shipwrecks randomly dispersed throughout. The King then ordered an investigation into how Sicily was supported in the water, and Cola Fish reemerged to report that the island rested on three columns, one of which was broken. The final inquiry commissioned by the King concerned Cola Fish himself: how far under water could marine man venture? And to demonstrate the reliability of the experiment, he was to bring back a cannonball fired from the Messina lighthouse for that very purpose. Cola accepted, he would carry out these orders if the King insisted, but he would never be seen again. The King did insist; Cola plunged into the sea after the cannonball, which sank rapidly in the water, found it in the deepest part of the ocean, picked it up, but when he raised his head to begin his ascent, he saw that the waters above him were firm and unmoving. He realized that the space he had come to was peaceful, silent and waterless. It was impossible to reach the waves again, impossible to swim. Cola ended his life there. That was the tale you had read in Benedetto Croce, filtered through countless variants, from Gualtiero Mapes to the pre–*Don Quixote* Spanish tradition, from the version collected by Athanasius Kircher for his *Mundus Subterraneus* to the one versified by Schiller. A man trapped at the bottom of the sea in a vast air pocket, this had always been the aspect which had made the deepest impression on you, and these were the fancies which flashed through your mind as you tumbled through three thousand feet in a matter of seconds; what exactly was it like to have water above and air beneath, to have everything topsy-turvy, upside down, but with one extra, unexpected margin for further survival? So, when the blood rushed back to your brain and you became yourself again, both Croce and the *Cunto de li Cunti* had made way for one single word, *overspeed,* the point at which velocity causes structural breakup.

"India Echo November, any problems?" broke in our Neapolitan Hegelian once again, "India Echo November!..." The most incongruous aspect was that unremarked detail of the underwater air pocket, highlighted in none of the standard versions of the tale; no one had thought it worthwhile to linger over that unprecedented reversal of conditions, scarcely any different from the condition you were in as you rolled around, kicking frantically like a baby in an effort to locate the pedals and interrupt the rotation of the plane, which had now gone into tailspin.

You cut back the engine, letting the plane go into nosedive, how much more could you lose?—very little, according to the altimeter. You pulled at the control column, gently, although your inclination was to grab it hard towards you, you pulled gently so as not to go into irreversible free fall, you prayed that the surfaces would grip the air. To you, everything seemed to be simultaneously accelerating and moving with painful slowness, and when the column reacted to your grip, you responded with incredulity, opening the throttle until the instruments recorded a still wavering stability and a near normal speed.

"India Echo November, you've gone and changed altitude again. Four hundred now. Any chance of you keeping us informed?" sighed Air Traffic Control over the radio.

"I'm sorry, Treviso. We've been through a bad patch of turbulence."

"Strong turbulence? Right. All OK, yes?"

"Yeah. Stabilized at...one thousand. Could we have a fresh qudimike?"

"One two zero," came the reply. "Climb to three thousand." After a pause, "Twenty-six miles from VOR."

"Copied. India Echo November."

Sunt etiam fluctus per nubila, as Lucretius had it, there are also waves in the clouds, which is why lightning is extinguished in the skies like red-hot metal dipped in water; you were flying through invisible airwaves and raindrops which the propeller downdraft crushed, dried instantly and spread out on the windscreen as though they were transparent, fast-flying insects. You regained altitude, flying into a less dense grey, you journeyed on in the opaque body of cloud; the nebulosity, as it increased, reflected flickering anti-collision strobe lights on the wingtips, flashbulbs for souvenir photos of clouds, snapped from their insides, and with you in the thick of it. Although without training in the subject, you managed to get the electronic equipment working, you watched the radio signals from ground which brought the instruments to life in a flurry of blips and blurs, and the radio signals from space, digital numbers in a calculator which questioned satellites and supplied answers in terms of compass degrees. Not that everything made sense to you, but you felt calmer and better protected, by both Air Traffic Control and the cosmos. The approach in QDM was a repetitive procedure, requiring you to make a radar call every two minutes, and to say "Treviso, India Echo November for a qudimike"; Air Traffic Control replied with three numbers which you immediately put into the gyrocompass, adjusting direction.

Meteorology always appeared to you a science of disappointment, not because the reality failed to match the forecasts, but because its ordered classifications, which seemed a guarantee of something quite precise and measurable, inevitably gave way to a continual, totally elusive flux. Perhaps meteorology was the science of both forecasting and disappointment. In your early days of flying, you kept yourself as far from clouds as a sailor from icebergs, but later, when you understood that they would be part of your landscape as an airman, you made an effort to get to know them, or at least recognize them, but not the way you had done as a boy with minerals and plants, or with declensions, endings and cases, because there was no definite image which corresponded to the definition of a cloud; the aeronautical handbooks were useful but too assertive, Aristotle too much the cosmogonist, and a cloud was never quite what it was supposed to be. The only one who had really understood and accepted this was Luke Howard, the Englishman who gave clouds their names. He was the first to decide they should be named *cirrus, cumulus, cirrostratus* or *cumulonimbus*. He alone had understood that a cloud is neither an object nor a state but a constant transition which should be described as such, and for this reason he entitled his book *On the Modifications of Clouds*. Goethe dedicated an ode to him.

"Treviso radar. India Echo November looking for a qudimike."

"India Echo November, your QDM's one one seven."

"Copied."

A new bearing, slightly more northerly. Howard's terminology in Latin would have read *Cirrus: nubes cirrata, tenuissima quae undique crescat* ("parallel, flexuous or diverging fibers, extensible in any or in all directions," in his own words). In this modification, the clouds seemed to have minimum density, maximum elevation and the greatest variety of extension; they began in the upper skies as the slenderest of threads, drew themselves out, attracted others at each side, produced yet others in a growth pattern which seemed at one moment totally random but seemed at others to be following a meticulously precise direction, perhaps parading silently before the moon. The modification of the *cirri* is to all appearances an immobile modification, but it is in fact linked to swirling movements in the atmosphere; in humid conditions, cirrus clouds might well descend from higher altitudes, changing into cirrostrati, *nubes extenuatae sub-concavae vel undulatae* ("horizontal or slightly inclined masses, attenuated towards a part or the whole of their circumference"). A fresh modification can be produced by the lowering of the cirri fibers, by their massing together in an unstable complex of mobile shapes, making them more compact at the center and more fragmented towards the extremities.

"Treviso radar. India Echo November requesting a qudimike."

"India Echo November, one one zero as requested. Fourteen miles from VOR. Maintain course."

In the one cloud, cirrostrati could alternate with cirrocumuli, *nubeculae densiores subrotundae et quasi in agmine appositae* ("small, well-defined roundish

masses, in close horizontal arrangement"), a modification produced by one cirrus, or a small group of
cirri, breaking up as a consequence of the dispersal of
the fibers into several more restricted masses, each well
rounded and distinct; the texture of the cirrus as such
would no longer be discernible, the change occurring
all at once in the inside, or progressively from one
extremity to the other; the new modification would
produce a beautiful sky, with numerous, different
clusters of tiny clouds which would then, in hot
weather, evaporate or modify once more into a cirrus
or cirrostratus.

"Treviso radar. India Echo November requesting
qudimike."

"India Echo November, one one zero the QDM.
On course for Charlie. Report back."

"Roger."

Words and clouds, Air Traffic Control's readings
coincided (you noted with surprise) with what, as you
struggled to steady the needles and blips of the radio-
beacon signals, was coming up on your own instruments, clouds and words, research into clouds had
been under way for thousands of years, while only
recently had it been possible to fly inside clouds, to see
them from inside; but the rub is that once inside a
thing it can no longer be seen, it has to be imagined
from the outside, so, as you passed through the now
abated storm at three thousand feet above earth, you
caught only muffled lightning flashes, making the
clouds seem like the storm's glowing innards. Had it
been a storm at sea, you would have had to endure
the howl and roar, but here, in your plane, you were

cocooned and cut off from the elements, you were the storm, you were caught in its eye; for you there was no more to it than a series of soundless bumps, sudden drops and automatic adjustments, overridden by the noise of the propeller. You tried to leave the cumuli behind you, *nubes cumulata, densa, sursum crescens* ("convex or conical heaps, increasing upwards from a horizontal base"), that is, the clouds appeared to be of denser structure, were formed in the lower atmosphere, were equipped with a nucleus around which the rest consolidated, had an unevenly shaped lower layer and were topped with cones and pinnacled spheres. Before raining, the cumulus swelled up to reveal a surface marked by jagged flakes and bulges; sometimes a cirrostratus would swiftly coil around the upper part, like the brim around the crown of a hat, leaving the pre-existing cumulus distinguishable and intact inside it. This was, however, a mutation of short duration, since the cirrostratus would quickly turn more dense and dispersed, so that while the upper part of the inner cumulus could spread out and flow into it, the base would proceed as before, allowing the convex bulges to move to a new position beneath and beside it. This in its turn permitted the formation of a huge cloud, the *cumulo-stratus, nubes densa, basim planam undique supercrescens, vel cuius moles longinqua videtur partim plana partim cumulata*—the type of cloud which you had in all probability blundered into—where the cumulus pierced the interstices of the clouds above, giving the whole, if seen on the horizon, if seen by Howard, the appearance of a snow-covered mountain range, dotted with peaks, darker buttresses, lakes, valleys, rocks and crags, rather than a cloud, a complete synthesis in the sky of the landscape.

"Treviso radar. India Echo November for a qudimike."

"India Echo November, your QDM's one zero eight. Drifting slightly to south. Nine miles from VOR."

Nine miles: that is, at current speed, two and a half minutes; you had further reduced speed, unwittingly, not so much because of the turbulence as because of an illusion that you needed room for maneuver, or evasion, in the face of some unexpected obstacle; be sincere, you still don't trust instruments, and perhaps not the Air Traffic Control people or the satellites either, so you keep to a speed just above the stalling speed you had dropped to earlier on. How odd that around the same time you had twice come across the same images of an airplane stalling: the identical photo taken in a wind chamber of a spiral of air whirling on a wing top had appeared both in aeronautical handbooks, where it was depicted as the most appalling of events, the worst that could befall a pilot and thus to be avoided at all costs, and in up-to-date physics textbooks, where it was exalted as a remarkable example of chaos theory; certainly you were honored that a stall was considered by contemporary thought as a "critical point phenomenon," and that in the white vapor indicating the separation of the flowing wisps of cloud and the wing top—a photographic reproduction of the uncontrollability of turbulence— some had seen the ancient consubstantiality, the ancient concurrence of order and disorder; oh yes, there was one part of you which participated enthusiastically in the wonder that a butterfly beating its wings in New York could lead to etc., etc.... You were a lover of chance and coincidence, but you were the one beating the wings, pilot; order and disorder, separated by no more than quantity, by a curve before which and beyond which lay the realm of the one and of the other, chaos containing order containing chaos, rather like the white, green and yellow curves in your instruments which indicated stalling speeds, the curve of speeds within which your airplane was an airplane, but under and over which it was so no longer. Your job was to remain lord and master of those tiny confines, assuming that your wish was to get to the VOR, and perhaps even to return home.

"India Echo November, you're over Charlie. Descend from three thousand to one thousand five hundred. Report when in visual contact with ground or water."

"Roger."

In no other place was the spoken word so vital as in the skies, nowhere else was it devoured with such greed. Flight had its own alphabet, a lesser alphabet like Braille or Morse, an alphabet with no ambition to coin words, a simple phonetic alphabet composed neither of symbols translating letters nor of letters making up words, but which used only common words to spell out, beyond all possibility of error, the letters of the everyday alphabet: a lexicon at the service of an alphabet and not vice versa: Bravo for B, Sierra for S, six people's names, Juliet, Charlie, Mike, Oscar, Romeo and Victor, two dances, the fox-trot and the tango, two nations, Quebec and India, one city, Lima, two ethnic groups, Yankee and Zulu, one hotel, one liqueur, one uniform, one month, November, to represent the rest, one clinical analysis, the X ray. A spoken alphabet, so ordered to deny anyone the liberty to indicate a letter by a favorite activity of their own, perhaps F for Flamenco rather than fox-trot, the dance which, together with the tango, had always been considered the only dance acknowledged by radio operators throughout the world. Although at the beginning this language had seemed to you overblown and extravagant, you had gradually come to appreciate its value; it had to be precise every time, since, uniquely, there would never be a second chance for correcting error or misunderstanding. The most unreal of languages, with the maximum of density in the minimum of words, embodying the maximum of imagination, each word having to designate instantaneously a geography of trajectories, positions, intentions, of starting points and destinations, as now, when Air Traffic Control mentions another flight coming up on your radio beacon, asks if you were listening, if you copied, if you understood. Words with consequences, then, dealing with matters of life and death and requiring a high quotient of intellectual honesty; any attempt at lying would immediately cause Air Traffic Control to abandon the procedural jargon and come out with a direct "You sure?" Your message had invariably the same structure—who you are, where you are coming from and going to, where you are when speaking, where you will call from next and when; the reply from Air Traffic Control was of the same standard type—I know where you are, I know where you are bound, this is your position and this is the position of other planes, here is what you have to do, here is where I am expecting you to check in next. Sometimes, talking into the radio in flight, the line would go dead, you stopped receiving replies, and there would be no knowing at which end the breakdown had occurred; you then found yourself obliged to issue blind messages, messages launched into the air, the procedure to be followed when, receiving no reply, not hearing a voice, you could not be sure if someone was hearing you and you were not receiving him, or if it was your radio that was no longer transmitting.

"India Echo November? Why have you not commenced descent?"

I'll tell you why. It's because to break through clouds or fog from above is always frightening, especially in the beginning, so it's easier to circle over the VOR, maintaining your altitude. You stare at the dots and hands on the instruments as they rotate or disappear, you want to be totally certain, the radio beacon is a platform of cement and aerials at sea level, situated on a strip of coastline, you will make a vertical, circle by circle, descent.

"Treviso radar, India Echo November. We're circling over Charlie."

"Go ahead, circle, circle..."

And you circled, circled, exiting from the clouds in concentric circles, as you had ascended so you would descend, five hundred feet a minute; clouds in painting had always had the function of linking or separating heaven and earth, a curtain or a lift, it all depended, someone might emerge from the clouds to speak, or someone might ascend from down there. What a problem clouds presented! When the Chinese wanted to paint them, they filled their mouths with white powder and blew on a sky previously sketched in ink on the page, as though the portrait had to be made of the same material as the subject.

"India Echo November, you back in Victor Mike Charlie?"

"India Echo November? Can you see...?" Air Traffic Control's voice rang out again.

You had eyes only for the altimeter, five hundred, four hundred, three hundred.

The sea appeared quite suddenly at the end of the last circle, and alongside it the city and your final destination, more glittering and bright than it had ever appeared to you before.

Flight Maneuvers

TO KNOW EVERYTHING, indeed more than everything, and to transform that knowledge into natural gestures which can be acted on instantly and instinctively, but not too instinctively; to have knowledge to the point that it becomes movement of the hand, sensitivity of the fingers to instruments and sensitivity of the body to positions in space, kinetics. To know, but not to know too much, and not to be oversure of that knowledge, because error, lying in wait for any display of cockiness, is always ready to pounce. Error was the pilot's speciality, and your discipline and chosen subject. If there was one expertise reserved for the pilot, it was expertise in error. What did you say your business was? Error, sir, nothing but error.

Words like "kinetics" would never have crossed Bruno's lips. He would never have spoken to you of such things, indeed would never have spoken of them at all, not to anyone, but would certainly have expected you to have a grasp of them. There was no inapplicable idea in the whole gamut from aerodynamic equations to advice to navigators, Notams read at the last minute before takeoff warning of possible temporary dangers; no idea at all however abstract or doltish, however remote in the recesses of memory, that might not be of use. There was no such thing as primary or secondary notions; there was no hierarchy in a pilot's knowledge, any more than in error itself; on the contrary, error took a strongly democratic and egalitarian view of guilt. From its point of view, neglect of a fundamental principle was in every sense equivalent to neglect of a trifling exception to the grammar of flight. There were, then, no primary or secondary errors; but you had a serendipitous flair for committing errors of both types, with equal success. In life, to choose the wrong wife or the wrong lift was conventionally viewed as being matters of varying gravity, but in piloting an aircraft an act of petty oversight, which in day-to-day life would rank with forgetting an umbrella, could, due to the obvious but decisive fact that in flight there can be no stopping, be fatal. There may be perfect reversibility in space, but not in time, so you could scarcely ever have a second chance at some failed procedure, or at some unsuccessful or overlooked maneuver. In no case would you have the liberty of stopping in midair to attend to something you should have seen to on the ground. It was your habit to try out the brakes as you lined up the plane for takeoff, because you would not have occasion to use them again until landing at your destination, and if you had failed to perform the due tests earlier on, it was only at that point, as you pushed down the pedals and the plane careered off the runway in spite of the pressure of your feet, that you would discover whether or not they were in working order. An aircraft had something ballistic about it, you could go anywhere, but the flight would in any case complete its own destiny, and that destiny was invariably earth-to-earth, irrespective of the bodily form in which you arrived.

Bruno could never be persuaded to talk about these matters, or if pressed, would reply with a few laconic verbs in the infinitive, and that only at table where the infinitives could be spaced out between silent mouthfuls. Bruno carried, etched in his mind, a detailed map of airports, flight paths and radio beacons, with another map superimposed on it, this time of the restaurants of Italy, with the result that during a flight, quite out of the blue, he was liable to announce, Let's land here—and that "here" would be a tiny airstrip scarcely identifiable in the surrounding grass, at Lugo di Romagna, at Thiene, at Massa Cinquale or at Busto Arsizio where he was born, but never far from the goal, which was a trattoria he was especially fond of. However, even a humble broth cooked by engineers on a primus stove in a hangar, on grey and rainy days, would arouse his interest but not disturb his silences. After the meal, once the rain passed, Bruno would move out of his office like a village elder, lean a seat against the side of a gas pump and sit there communing with the clouds and the air. You, meantime, were left to walk the deserted apron, waiting for the sky to clear, losing yourself in lengthy imaginary conversations which this impossible relationship prevents you from having man to man; you would say to him, Look

Bruno, when you, in midair, pull back the levers and say calmly, "Engine emergency," and reach your hand over my control column to switch off the magneto and stop the propeller, you leave me only a moment to stare, petrified, at that immobile sword on the horizon, before I set my mind to doing what requires to be done. The silence in the cockpit is noisier than a voice, but you don't speak, you don't even check my movements, you sense them from our trim, from the way I maneuver to bring you slowly in to land, from how I let the plane and our bodies drift in the search for the best angle, from how I give rein or else rein in. During afternoons like this, while awaiting takeoff, I go over in my mind all the stalls, turns and spins, and perhaps I am now better equipped to attempt them, look at the loops and spins I can master now! Every evening, I am the last to leave the airfield, taking away with me all that I acquired during a day of practice in falls and lost equilibrium, or if you prefer of equilibrium in extreme situations. I would like to be able to apply this equilibrium somewhere else, Bruno—are there such things as life maneuvers?—but will I ever be able to talk to you about it, and if so how? There you are seated against a gas pump like a cat beside a radiator, your arms folded, staring at the cement of the crumbling parade area with roots and herbs breaking the surface all around; it is an old, tired airfield, who knows what you're waiting for on afternoons like this. At times, in these old airfields, all those who ever failed to reach their destination seem to be huddled there, now invisible, luggage clasped in hand, waiting for relatives to collect them, exactly as once, who

knows when, those relatives had awaited with growing despair the arrival of the loved ones who would
never appear. But this is only one of many dreadful
instances of never meeting again. If I had ever managed to discuss such innocuous hallucinations with
you, Bruno, they would surely have found their way
onto my medical record, or perhaps not. Do you ever
think of what it would be like if it were possible to
behave in life as in flying, of what would happen if
the same reversibility could be produced in life? In
flying, everything is based on the circularity of the
compass, every point can be viewed in two opposing
perspectives, every calculation in navigation has its opposite calculation, each reference point constitutes a
choice not of value but of position, and one easily overturned; we navigate by distance from, with instruments which indicate the route travelled from our
starting point, and we navigate by approach to, with
instruments which home in on the destination, on the
point of arrival. In flying, our teleology functions
equally well in reverse; it does not designate exclusively movement to but also movement, or distancing,
from, even if our sensation is not of a mere "past" but
rather of a lead wire, a "track," starting somewhere
behind us and hauling us in some direction as it un-
winds; teleology is that red needle I see every day
turning in the instrument glass, flying about as it pur-
sues radials in all directions, moving from a point I
am at complete liberty to consider the point of departure or arrival. The needle will carry the word "to"
or "from," everything is relative, moveable words for
departure or approach, and when it does not indicate

"to" or "from," the needle says simply "off," too distant to be able to pick up any signal. I would relish
the liberty of freely choosing—in life too—a beam
and travelling along it, no matter whether "to" or
"from;" a signal from a radio beacon can, in any case,
go in only one direction, from its own source outwards, from the radio beacon itself towards the infinite, like a coastal warning light; the signal is, then,
bound to indicate origin, it can never be other than a
"from" signal, so I could wing my way towards it,
except that, in such a case, the needle's indications
would be inverted, or as you would say, Bruno, "anti-
instinctive." North is north, although it is not the only
one, it is simply a reference point, every degree on the
compass enjoys equal dignity, every spot on the earth's
surface is simultaneously journey's end and journey's
beginning, transposed from time to time, as the occasion demands. If I could only accept that all that
matters is the individual section, or "stretch" as you
prefer to name all journeys, and could reject all forms
of nostalgia for departure or arrival; or else if only I
could face the knowledge that departure and arrival
can often be the same thing, can coincide. Perhaps,
Bruno, that is ultimately why we fly, to gain that mea-
gre satisfaction which can be derived, on each occasion, from departure-cum-arrival, from arriving in the
very act of departure, and from the idea of having
accomplished at least this. It seems that something has
been done, even if that something is to be measured
in mere miles. (All this has been said in so many
books, by so many experts and scribblers with no experience of aeronautics, but I have never managed to

apply it in life without a residue of pain and nostalgia. These are matters which can be savored in the mind but never assimilated in the depths of one's being; only when flying do they come to me naturally, because they are the very structure and necessity of flight, nor could it be otherwise.)

You know, Bruno, there are so many things I delude myself I could learn from here, from this old airfield; here every situation has its set procedure, you demonstrate it, or leave it to each of us to pick it up and repeat it until it becomes instinctive, but not too instinctive. Take night flights: you taught us that in observing city lights, or outlines or prominent, illuminated points it was essential to keep looking down or to one side, like bashful or coquettish maidens, so that things would appear as they are and not as they present themselves when viewed from off-center; in night flights, you said, resist the temptation to stare at the lights. To see things in their real dimensions in poor light or at night, it is advisable to take a sideways look, to use what you call "peripheral vision." I have no trouble doing that in flight, Bruno, but in life? I continue to look at things head-on, frontally, and am crushed by the vision; I stare at it transfixed, so that one scene, one memory or one obsession blots out the entire panorama. Somewhere there must surely be a periphery to vision from which everything can be brought back into focus, a maneuver of the eye which allows it to outflank obstacles and restore a sense of proportion, but for me it has never been easy to find. (I am starting to think that being crushed in that way may serve a purpose, may be of cumulative value, may make a rhythm, but, aeronautically, operationally, you could never agree.) In flying, there is scarcely anything direct; to be centered and immediate, everything requires to have been previously adjusted and compensated for, so that if it is in the center, its position is due to a deliberate, prior decentering and displacement. If I fly into gusts or crosswinds I must set the nose into the wind, into the direction the wind is coming from, veering perhaps as much as thirty or forty degrees off course; the direction is no longer the one I wish to follow, but it is only by navigating off course that I can stay on course and keep to my flight path. And this decentering caused by wind patterns at height is only part of a more complex, careful dislocation: to get to my destination, I navigate according to the difference between three norths—magnetic north, geographic north and the north given by the cockpit compass as influenced by the metals in the aircraft itself. Each north has to be added to, or subtracted from, the others, from my route, as well as from the final number which I will follow on the gyroscopes, wagering everything on that number, like a gambler. To reach the destination, I set the nose in a wholly different direction, following an imaginary route which goes somewhere else, to a place which exists exclusively in terrestrial magnetism, in calculation and in the wind. I have no other means at my disposal for coinciding with my destination.

Bruno remained silent, a sky of dark clouds rolled over the airfield, in the hangars the clash of beaten metal provided a temporary recall to reality, behind the tinted glass windows of the control tower it was just possible to make out the profiles of the individual operators, dragging on their cigarettes as they waited. The sluggishness of the afternoon seemed to have cut activities adrift one from the other, reducing them to a minimum, leaving each one enveloped in its own specific silence; the silence of the uniformed customs officers at the barroom door, wordlessly gazing at the briefcase to which someone has attached a computer printout "Before putting your mouth in motion, make sure your brain is in gear" (it must be this fear that makes you remain silent), or the silence of Bruno with his arms folded and his head bowed, or your more garrulous silence as you walk up and down in front of him without finding the words to say what you want to say, for instance that all this forward planning and calculating is not in your nature. Bruno, I would prefer to deal with a flight minute by minute, seeing to all that is to be done, facing up to occurrences rather than going over each flight long before clambering on board, and having then, in flight, to be always in imagination some miles or some minutes ahead of the plane. In life, once, I knew instinctively what I should be doing, but I forced myself to carry out a slow tour of all the opportunities open to me, only to return to the one which had attracted me at the outset; but whether following instinct or reason, everything always went wrong, especially when I was convinced I had done the right thing, so it's as well to make instinctive mistakes, to make immediate, impulsive mistakes, and at least get it over with. However, in flight, instinct is another debatable matter, something which needs to be worked on, contradicted and reversed.

"Anti-instinctive" maneuvers is your term for dealing with, for instance, a stall, when you feel a wing going down, the plane begin to vibrate, and an alarm or a mechanized voice in the cabin saying over and over again, Stall! Stall! Stall! The voice will be in English, the official language used in aeronautics, even for bad news. At that moment your heart will tell you to pull at the control column, to tug hard and keep up the already dropping nose; if you do that, you may be following instinct, but the wing will definitively lose its grip on the air, instantly transforming the aircraft and all of us inside it into a deadweight. There are many reasons why a plane goes into stall—lack of attention, an inaccurate or incomplete mental grasp of conditions, external events, like icing—but the only way to get out of it is to let yourself fall, to defy every impulse and assist the stall, to push the nose down and go with the plunge until reaching the point where speed, and air, are regained. The same applies with spin; once you go into a spin, your first inclination is to start turning the column the opposite way from the rotation, then to twist it frantically in any direction which will interrupt the spinning motion, but this only causes the wing to lose the little lift it has retained, leaving no hope of getting out of the spin. Never use the control column, the catechism instructs, restrain instinct, the spin must be managed by the pedals and tail rudder, the last to lose efficiency in such circumstances. There are many reasons why a plane goes into stall or spin—lack of attention, error, loss of lift, an inexact appreciation of one's own position, or perhaps position in relation to others, an undue concentration on one aspect, causing every image, every meaning, every direction to be fixed by that one aspect to the exclusion of all others. In life too there are those emergency moments when the instincts cry out for immediate, resolute reactions, moments of stall when we strive to continue climbing and to keep upright at height when the only way out would be to let ourselves drift, moments when we gaze at things full-on and go for the heart when the one reasonable trajectory would carry us off center, towards an outer edge which, once reached, should be proceeded along gingerly but undeviatingly, and other moments when we find ourselves caught up in a headlong spin and seize wildly at every available lever, succeeding only in making the spin all the more uncontrollable. You, Bruno, would undoubtedly urge "anti-instinctive maneuvers"! but there is, in life, no knowing whether one is always capable of doing the opposite, nor of telling whether an individual really wants a way out; instinct and noninstinct can be intertwined or inverted, and the left has its own left which is not always the right. In fact, in aviation too there is a mysterious zone, the only one with any resemblance to all this, a zone of extreme conditions, the aerodynamic zone where piloting is done by inverted commands, where the relationship between velocity and power attains a threshold beyond which, by means of those "inverted commands," you pass to a different regime, where if you wish to climb you must push the control column down and if you wish to descend you must pull it towards you. It is not easy to understand, any more than it is easy to recognize immediately that you have penetrated those zones. Rarely do you acknowledge that what is asked of you is the exact opposite of what is wanted of you, that the real question is the inverse of its formulation; in flight, if you realize in time what is going on, you can regain control, whereas in love, even if you were capable of recognizing early on that you were falling into the realm of "inverted requests," and even if you had in your turn the power to invert your replies and gestures, neither you nor she would be any more capable of escape; there is no exit from love through inverted questioning, since to produce the correct reply to an upside-down question does nothing to remove the pain or the problem which overturned the question in the first place.

We fly by mental images, Bruno, choosing between them at every moment, visualizing positions in relation to a no-longer-visible earth and sky, positions which we imagine through the exercise of, if you will excuse the term, a finely honed, exquisitely gauged imagination, and there is no more to it; small hallucinations prompted by the instruments, developed one after the other throughout the flight, hallucinations which do not give rise to dreams, release or to any sort of description, but simply to a maneuver, to a work of the hands needed for progress to some destination. Certainly, the finely honed imagination has as its support mechanisms the panel of instruments which little by little replace the real world, the world outside the windscreen which can often be no longer seen. Of the six instruments essential for piloting an airplane, each one describes a "truth" directly, with at least another two doing so indirectly; each instrument is in turn of prime importance for one maneuver and of secondary importance for others, as happens in a Chinese game, or in infinite combinations of the same elements, or in those stories where each character knows only one part of the final truth. I speak of "truth," Bruno, only because you insist that instruments must be believed absolutely, but it is not without a tremor that, as I break through the clouds, I switch to considering as "truths" some boxes of metal and plastic mounted on an instrument panel; it requires each time a little act of faith and forgetfulness.

Here even emergencies become a question of habit, part of a discipline: how to make something utterly dramatic and terminal into something normal and routine. The realization dawns very quickly that while it initially seems there is nothing more to be done, there remains the speeding time itself that can be stretched out by a second-by-second concentration on each individual one of the seconds that make up that time, a cramped space that can be extended by being subdivided into acts and operations each of which is worth meters in the sky and feet of maintained altitude. Between being and not being airborne there is a no-man's-land of seconds, miles, altitude, and that is our territory, Bruno, there we work, there we have our being. There's all the time in the world, you say, casually switching off the engine in midair, and while I sweat over it, you ask, Suppose it was an engine fire instead of a straightforward breakdown? I give the handbook reply, Fuel tanks off, pump off, make no attempt to start her up again, etc., etc., I go into all the details of the maneuver to be followed, while executing a completely different one to get us out of the mess you have got us into, but do you know what I really want to say, Bruno? If it were to happen, I think it would all depend. No really, it would all depend. If there were passengers on board, I'd damn my soul if it were the price of bringing them down safely, but if I were on my own, if I had the utter certainty that I had one minute left and not a second more, I wouldn't spend it that way. I genuinely don't know if I'd strive to the last, I think I'd prefer to throw in the towel, focus on the people I've loved, apologize to them for shortcomings, rather than take my leave tugging frantically at levers on an aircraft flight deck.

The pilot's lore has an objective, which is not the immediate one of piloting an aircraft, but primarily that of producing images of the state of things and of their continual advance, as well as of mastering appropriate behavior, which must be so deeply assimilated that it will appear natural and spontaneous in an experience where everything is unnatural. This, Bruno, is second nature to you, but you will not speak of it, any more than you will speak of anything else. The naturalness of the unnatural requires special care and maintenance, it must be constantly used, like a path through vegetation which will be overgrown the moment it ceases to be trodden. To allow it to fall into disuse means to lose it bit by bit. A pilot's knowledge is an unending apprenticeship, and this is the point of those infinite checks which you, like every other aeronautic authority, make us undergo, irrespective of age or seniority, and is probably why everything has its own training course, proceeds to its own license.

Everything has its expiry date, Bruno, here everything has a fixed time span, here everything dies periodically; there is no means of renewal except by demonstrating that you made use of that learning by putting it into practice hour after hour, day after day, month after month, year after year in flights, hours airborne, hours in command. The learning of which you are master, Bruno, is more subject to reassessment than any other, and perhaps the only one liable to be revoked at any time unless it is shown that it has been applied sufficiently, and undoubtedly the only one to carry in large print its own sell-by-date, like milk.

To assist me in this ever-shifting borderland, I have a little book of prayers, a minor book, just as the guides and manuals I enjoyed as a boy were minor works. Every morning as I go up in my plane, I first open my breviary. Each subject in the text is arranged in question-and-answer format, so that it ought to be recited in twos, but it can be adapted for one, as more and more frequently happens. The one person has to be ready to take both parts:

> *Master switch?* On.
> *Anticollision beacon?* On.
> *Flaps?* Ten degrees.
> *Parking brake?* On.
> *Radios?* Tuned and checked.
> *Instruments?* Set as required.
> *Trimmer?* Neutral.

As with other forms of prayer, this one too has a part for the hands, to do with the switches. Further, just as there are prayers for each moment of the day, so each phase of flight has a propitiatory liturgy of its own: prior to switch-on, prior to taxying, after takeoff, at cruising speed, for final approach, for landing, for parking, and of course, those special prayers for emergencies whose pages in the breviary are edged in red so they can be flicked open instantly, should the need arise. All praise to the checklist, Bruno, a modest but enormously valuable book, but a book which, fortunately or unfortunately, none can call on for the maneuvers and emergencies of life.

These are the things you would have liked to say to him, and it seems to you that possibly, just possibly, this could be the right time, now, in this afternoon of endless waiting, when the barometer refuses to move to "Fine" and even a fool could see that you will not be taking off, possibly, just possibly, you could break your silence and talk to him about these things. You move up to the gas pump. Bruno is asleep, as he has been for some time, so deeply asleep that he has not even noticed the light drizzle which has started to fall, sending a few drops coursing down his bald skull.

Unreported Inbound Palermo

IF THIS WERE a chapter on Ustica,* it would have to
be the history of the aircraft. It would be the history
of an aircraft which plunged to the bottom of the sea
only to reemerge from the waters, a creature of metal
which sank and rose again, as in a mythical tale, a
being created for the air which ended in water, water
believed by humankind to be the worst of all things,
worse than earth or mountain, brutal by contrast, water occasions greater fear, three thousand meters under
the surface of the sea, three thousand seven hundred,
and then raised from the sea piece by piece, and every
piece reassembled with infinite care around the make-
shift structure, the simulacrum, as that unreal skeleton

---

* Associated with the name Ustica is one of the most mysterious incidents and one of
the greatest scandals in recent Italian history. On the night of June 27, 1980, a DC-9,
owned by the airline Itavia, while on a scheduled flight from Bologna to Palermo, exploded in the air and fell into the sea near the island of Ustica, not far from Palermo.
All eighty-one of the passengers and crew on board were killed. The truth about what
occurred was covered up by the secret service and the military elite. The victims' relatives
petitioned the government for seven years until the wreckage was salvaged from a depth
of 3,700 meters. Despite much resistance and little help from international authorities,
the Italian magistrate continues to investigate the theory that the plane was hit by a
missile or exploded by a bomb.

in the hangar is called, every piece attached in faithful reconstruction of the original aircraft. The history might be entitled *The Itigis*, as if it were the tale of some ancient people or of trees older than time and not of pieces of metal which crumbled and were reassembled. In the air, on the sea bed and finally on land. And when is the next departure?

"Bologna Ground, ready to start up engines."

"Itavia Eight Seven Zero cleared, temperature twenty-four degrees, stop time on the hour. Do you have the latest weather report?" and in the silence of the hangar, at nights, a slow drip-drip could be heard, as though even now when the aircraft was on dry land, the sea, after pressing down for years on the metal molecules, was continuing its slow withdrawal, drop by drop, and as though the aircraft would never be completely free of its grip.

"Itavia Eight Seven Zero, cleared for Palermo via Florence, Ambra one three, climb and maintain flight level one nine zero. Repeat and report ready to take off." The Itigis, I-TIGI, India Tango India Golf India, would be a first-person narrative related by the metal itself, a being which was first an aircraft, then finished on the sea bed and rose again, and was once again, later, an aircraft, a creature of reconstituted metal: but between its before and after as an aircraft, not everything can resume its place, for around eighty people, passengers and crew, are missing.

"Itavia Eight Seven Zero, takeoff at eight, contact Padua Information."

"Itavia Eight Seven Zero with Padua information, Bologna goodbye," an event which moves backwards enveloping itself within itself, as in those film sequences where a bottle of milk shatters in a thousand pieces causing the thick liquid to spurt in all directions, and then each shard, reconstituting itself, flashes back through time and space into the place it had occupied, with even the liquid flowing back into the bottle drop by drop. But in the unmaking and remaking of the event, something is missing and will be missing forever.

"Good evening Padua, Itavia Eight Seven Zero here."

"Itavia Eight Seven Zero, proceed as cleared, report Florence." Sweeping over the ocean bed, the underwater camera made out five letters of the alphabet, I-TIGI, painted in black on the underside of the left wing, and there could be no further doubt, the Itigis were there, the tail four kilometers ahead of the pilot's cabin.

"Good evening, Rome, Itavia Eight Seven Zero here."

"Good evening to you, Eight Seven Zero. Go ahead."

"Eight Seven Zero over Florence, flight level one six zero climbing one nine zero. Estimate Bolsena at three four."

"Itavia Eight Seven Zero, roger. Squawk ident one two three six. Cleared to Palermo via Bolsena, Puma, Latina, Ponza, Ambra one three."

"One two three six squawking. Eight Seven Zero ready for further climb."

"Itavia Eight Seven Zero, radar contact. Climb initially to flight level two three zero. Other company traffic precedes you, six miles ahead, flight level two five zero."

"Rome, traffic in sight."

The Itigis were lying there, not far from a Roman ship with a cargo of glass, a vessel with seventeenth-century cannons, a Second World War Messerschmitt fighter, items from the memories of transport, an involuntary sea-bed museum.

"Itavia Eight Seven Zero, turn right, heading one seven zero. With traffic in sight cleared flight level two nine zero. Resume own navigation to Bolsena passing flight level two six zero."

"Eight Seven Zero up to flight level two nine zero, leaving one nine zero." From the beginning the sonar echo traced on the plotters the outline of uncertain, abstract magnetic masses, with the probability ranging through high, medium and low that it was not a geological object but an object of human construction; later, in full view of the cameras, every piece became a numbered object, and finally, at the moment the cranes lowered it, dripping water, onto the deck, its nature was established as an exhibit.

"Rome, Eight Seven Zero passing flight level two four five with traffic in sight. Cleared to turn left?"

"Affirmative, Itavia Eight Seven Zero. Proceed Bolsena."

To the east of the route, since without warning the aircraft veered to the east and so plunged into the sea (who would have believed that the cardinal points existed even under the sea?), were found the two engines, the one a quarter of a mile from the other; another mile to the east lay the cabin and wings; a further mile and a half off the trailing rudder; another two miles to the east the stern section of the fuselage and a large portion of the left wing, which had sheared off not on impact but due to extreme acceleration during descent; further still to the east a fuel tank, which had got there from somewhere or other; and finally the fuselage end plate, the six rear windows on the right, the six rear windows on the left.

"Good evening Rome, Eight Seven Zero here."

"Eight Seven Zero calling?"

"Yes, good evening, this is Eight Seven Zero maintaining two nine zero over Puma."

"Roger, Eight Seven Zero, proceed Latina-Ponza."

Everything at the rear would finish up forward, and vice versa; the Itigis, whatever hurtled them into the sea, had arranged themselves on the ocean floor along a corridor of debris almost ten kilometers in length, in the reverse of the order in which they had been flying at that moment. Every little detail was a work of deduction, the in-flight instruments as much as the rugs and carpet, neatly sheared off at the fourth row of seats. What can objects know about plots and actions? What do they know about ringleaders and accomplices? The objects are simply there. This should be the history of an airplane, because an airplane knows its history—how many people in this world know its history? In the absence of words, it would be the history of things: history of metal, metal sinning and sinned against; the fuselage knows what has produced unequal local disintegration just forward of the tailplane, the left fin of the stabilizer knows what opened a cross-shaped incision on its edge, just as the underside of the right flap certainly knows what perforated it and knows the nature of the tiny iron pellets located inside the metal sheets, the left side door knows what ripped away the external coating (simply designated "skin" in the inventory), the wrenched-off rivets know if they were detached by the speed of descent or by the force of a strike.

"Good evening, Rome. Eight Seven Zero here."

"Good evening, Eight Seven Zero, maintain flight level two nine zero, report on Ambra one three Alpha."

"Yes, listen, is Ponza out of action as well?"

"Sorry?"

"It's like padding through a graveyard this evening. South of Florence, there's hardly a beacon in operation."

"Afraid so, nearly everything's down tonight, including Ponza. What's your heading now?"

"We're maintaining heading one nine five."

"OK, maintain one nine five. With present heading you'll arrive some miles south of Ponza."

"Good, thanks."

"But look, you're only going to be able to maintain heading one nine five for another twenty miles or so, no more, there's a strong westerly wind, at your level it'll reach one hundred to one twenty knots."

"Yes, we've done our own calculations, and it must be something of that order."

The frame of the toilet door knows what flattened it into that shape, whether it was a shock wave while still in flight or the rudder crashing into the cabin on impact with the sea and crushing everything in its path, the rug in row five knows what ripped it apart, each piece of metal or plastic or fabric knows which other object, which splinter, and of what, reduced it to its present state.

"The Eight Seven Zero here, can we have...two five zero as level?"

"Affirmative. You can descend right away."

"Thank you, we're leaving two nine zero."

The Itigis did not all make their return at the same time but one by one (did the pieces left down below feel abandoned in the meantime?), first the cockpit with the nosewheel welded onto it, the right wing, the left engine, parts of the cabin, the front service hatch, some bulkheads from the baggage hold, the voice recorder, seats, life jackets, assorted tiny fragments. In this way, the aircraft in the hangar was re-formed in time, the crates were opened as they were brought in, the parts laid out on the cement, the items identified, the large tailplane assembled on the bearings, and for the cabin they began with the formers and battens of the structure, just as they had originally done in the factory.

"Itavia Eight Seven Zero, you've got Ponza three miles to the right, so for Palermo you're more or less on track."

"Much obliged, we're close to flight level two five zero."

"Perfect, Eight Seven Zero, in any case report as soon as you receive Palermo VOR."

"Yes, we've already tuned Papa Alpha Lima, and everything's OK. And we have the Ponza DME."

"Perfect. So normal navigation to Palermo. Maintain two five zero, and report on Alpha."

Who knows what emotions those who did that work will have had to keep in check (and what modest comfort they may have derived from thinking that work is work, or that they were in some way engaged in a "search for the truth")? Each item was given its tab, the maintenance manuals and the construction diagrams helped slot everything into its proper place and, in the early stages, each item hung with its label from the trestlework frame alongside the empty spaces which marked the missing pieces. As the aircraft resumed its shape and it became clear what was there and what was not, and where the destruction was more and where less complete, it became possible to read the aircraft as though it were the fragment of a palimpsest, each piece contributing to one possible reading of what had occurred, the right flank much more wracked with pain than the other, the metal not rusted even in the cracks, the company colors still seemingly fresh, the black stains of the engine air exhaust still visible; except that each piece no longer fitted with the others, because each clung to its own history, or its own deformity.

"Eight Seven Zero is on Alpha."

"Roger, slightly right of track, let's say . . . four miles. But look, radar service terminates here. Contact Rome Aerovie on one two eight point eight for further transmissions."

"Thanks for everything. Good night."

"Good night, Eight Seven Zero."

When the pieces were brought together, matched and refitted after all those years and miles of distance and separation, at first glance it was difficult to comprehend what had occurred, even if each part conserved the memory of it, because the aircraft in its present state is not as it was when resting on the sea bed, and it is on that arrangement, on that sea chart of debris, that any reading and interpretation should begin. The aircraft had either disintegrated in flight, leaving each piece to follow its own private parabola from twenty-five thousand feet to zero, or else it had plummeted headlong, engines dead, tearing itself apart on impact, and in that case it was the impact and nothing but the impact which was responsible for each and every injury, and the air and sea currents which were responsible for the drift.

"Rome, good evening, Itavia Eight Seven Zero."

"Good evening Itavia Eight Seven Zero, ahead."

"One hundred and fifteen miles for Papa Romeo Sierra, maintaining flight level two five zero."

"Roger, Itavia Eight Seven Zero, can you give us an estimate for Raisi?"

"Eight Seven Zero estimating Raisi around one three."

"Roger Eight Seven Zero, cleared to Raisi VOR, no delay expected. Report descent."

"No delay to Raisi. Will report descent."

"That's correct."

Perhaps out of respect, the passenger seats were never reassembled; the interior of the aircraft was a gangway laid out on the framework of the original flooring, as far as it could be reconstructed, and on it the carpet had been laid, and above the whole complex there was a tunnel made up of the cabin, left open fore and aft.

"Itavia Eight Seven Zero, when ready cleared to flight level one one zero. Report leaving two five zero and passing one five zero... Itavia Eight Seven Zero?"

At intervals in the hangar the families would gather around the Itigis to give vent to their pain or to give an account of the actions undertaken to obtain justice and knowledge of the truth, and on such occasions, the Itigis, after being a scheduled flight, after being wreckage lost, recovered and reassembled, became a monument to the dead. It would have been, for anyone observing in ignorance of the history, for anyone chancing upon those poor people assembled in a hangar around a patchwork airplane, an image of utterly incomprehensible anguish, all the more so since, on such occasions, the gangways inside the aircraft were no longer walked by experts but by police officers, authority figures and some photographers.

"Itavia Eight Seven Zero, do you read?"

In time the final pieces—the final fragment of a batten, the final stringer piece, the final section of riveted lining—all turned up and the Itigis were almost completely reunited, almost. And when is the next departure?

"Itavia Eight Seven Zero, Rome here, do you read?"

The flight recorder came to light, as did the last of the life jackets, the last of the oxygen masks, the frame of the forward door with porthole into the pilot's cabin, one fuel pump, one longeron with lining and rivets, one foldaway stool and one door with circular handle—"Itavia Eight Seven Zero, Rome...? Itavia Eight Seven Zero, Rome here...do you read?"—one electrical box, three hydraulic pipes, one crushed rod, one cockpit instrument, one jack with spring, one seat with safety belt—"Itavia Eight Seven Zero, do you read?...Itavia Eight Seven Zero, Rome here do you read?"—one piece of light-blue plate steel with instrument attached, one section of wing with valves and pipes, one black electrical/electronic box, one Plexiglas window, one piece of fuselage structure with mounting containing the word "Douglas," one piece of black casing with attached tubing, one grey-green container with electrical wiring—"Air Malta Seven Five Eight, this is Rome Control," "Rome go ahead," "Air Malta Seven Five Eight, please, try to call for us, try to call for us Itavia Eight Seven Zero, please," "Roger, sir... Itavia Eight Seven Zero...Itavia Eight Seven Zero, this is Air Malta charter Seven Five Eight, do you read? Itavia Eight Seven Zero...Itavia Eight Seven Zero, this is Air Malta charter Seven Five Eight, do you read...do you read?...Rome, negative contact with Itavia Eight Seven Zero"—another two windows with emergency exit handle, the notice bearing the illuminated sign "Emergency Exit," a further piece of fuselage with red paint, another white piece of fuselage with light-blue interior bent around white exterior, a burnt transformer with cable, a fragment of the de-icing line, some pages of the flight manual, a piece of external covering scorched by friction, one instrument without dial—"Itavia Eight Seven Zero, Itavia Eight Seven Zero, this is Rome Control, do you

read? ... Itavia Eight Seven Zero, Itavia Eight Seven
Zero, Rome Control, do you read?"—one hoist with
static discharger, one piece of Y-shaped ventilation
pipe, one cabin window, one frame for pulley support,
the rear stairway, the end section of the left wing, one
white dividing panel, one electrical fuse box with lid,
various battens and traverse frames, the galley, one
fragment of cabin with toilet flush mechanism, one
toilet seat— "Air Malta, this is Rome." "Rome go
ahead, this is Air Malta." "OK, sir, we have Itavia
Eight Seven Zero unreported inbound Palermo,
please, please try to call for us Itavia Eight Seven Zero,
try to call for us Itavia Eight Seven Zero," "Alitalia
Eight Seven Zero?" "Itavia, sir, Itavia, Itavia Eight
Seven Zero," "Roger ... Itavia Eight Seven Zero,
Itavia Eight Seven Zero this is Air Malta. Do you
read? Itavia Eight Seven Zero, do you read? ... do you
read? ..."

Do you read?

Double Takeoff at Dawn

THERE IS UNIVERSAL agreement that it was a beautiful July day, a day not made for warfare, the sea and sun of Bastia on the right, the line of hills on the left and straight ahead the runway of closely mown grass, yellowing and scented in the heat. Lieutenant Duviez pulled shut the canopy of the plane and slid down from the wing. Antoine de Saint-Exupéry switched on his radio and said: "Colgate from Dress down number six, may I taxi and take off?" He had no love for the radio, belonging as he did to an age when the radio was unknown, nor for the English language. He had recently returned from an American trip where he had repaid the triumph of his books with a refusal to speak a word in any language other than French. That morning he was in Corsica, where his right to use his own tongue was not in dispute, but the airplane which was about to take off was American, the squadron was Franco-American, being made up of all that was left of the great strategic reconnaissance unit Groupe II/33 de Grande Reconnaissance, with the addition of a few USA pilots and men from camera repair. Ground Control was also American, their radio call sign was *Colgate*, like the toothpaste. "Colgate from Dress down number six, permission to taxi and take off?" It was also the one morning when Gavoille, Captain René Gavoille, whom he had described in *Pilote de Guerre* as France's best, was not there to dress him in his thermic overall, to place him in his cockpit like a bear in a cage, to tie his straps, to check oxygen cylinder, revolver and camera switches in the belly of the plane, and give him last-minute advice. Two hours later, on arriving at the airstrip, Gavoille would be upset at that little act of treachery of Saint-Exupéry's in taking off before he got there, and a further two hours on he would regret not having himself carried out a minor act of treachery at the expense of his friend, an act of treachery that morning already agreed upon with the American High Command: the treachery of revealing to him an important secret, like the date of the landing in Provence, so as to invoke the regulation preventing him from undertaking further sorties because of the risk of his being captured and talking. But what could Gavoille have done? The other would have paid no heed, would have been loud in his protests; Gavoille recalled all too clearly one evening a short time before, when they had wept together and Saint-Exupéry had begged to be allowed to fly again and had finally entrusted him with the enormous manuscript of *Citadelle*, from which he had, years previously, read some pages to Benjamin Crémieux and Drieu La Rochelle.

"OK number six, you can taxi and take off," said

the controller. The airman Charles Suty, a boy who, to escape call-up in the Vichy Republic, had taken refuge in North Africa and joined the II/33, removed the chocks from the landing gear. Saint-Exupéry put the engines full on and released the brakes. The airplane began its takeoff run, the hills and sea of Bastia, even the runway itself began to race forward as Antoine de Saint-Exupéry, Tonio or Saint-Ex, lifted his shadow from this earth for the last time.

0715 HOURS, HEADING 243°, 7000 FEET. MIST.

There follows a brief journey towards a long story, a story of flight, narration and childhood, but also of a civil and philosophical passion for companionship and for oneness with the earth, of a few men from the thirties and forties, some still alive, of the mystery of a writer who in all probability crashed at sea, and of coincidences, which govern everything. The journey, mine, could well begin here, seven thousand feet above the Po delta, with the heading of the aircraft pushed very slightly off course by a light wind, a southerly wind, a genial, gentle sirocco such as could be picked up only by electronic apparatus and compasses, which every so often deviate a degree or two from the set course and seem ready to forge ahead in that direction until pressure of the foot, or a slight trim to the left, brings them back within the agreed range, or rather, so as to offset the effect of the wind, to something under it. A glance over the instruments is no different from the round of rooms made by a butler last thing at night. Since I am that butler, it would be difficult for me to attribute some heroic or mystical sense to flight; flight is no more than a science of doing, a matter of errors and corrections, of position and behavior. At least that is how it is today, perhaps it was different when Antoine de Saint-Exupéry made his night flights over the Andes to deliver the mail in Patagonia, or was Aéropostale's station chief in Juby in the Sahara, or fighter pilot over Arras or Grenoble, other times, heroic times, today that heroism would make no sense, and neither, fortunately, would the grand rhetoric that often accompanied it. On this July morning, no one takes voluntary risks; on the contrary, I keep things in order so as to ensure that the C172 of which I am butler glides peacefully along airway Red 22. If this were a sea voyage, I would be speaking of waves and the ship; if a journey on foot of the sort I used to undertake as a boy I would be talking of shoes, weariness and the countryside; but now after takeoff over the lagoon, the Po valley down below is invisible under an all-enveloping mango jelly, the horizon high and blurred in the heat mist, while the events of the journey at this moment amount to no more than an occasional touch on the instruments, done with the delicacy with which one might straighten up a painting on a wall after it had been dusted. I busy myself with the Chioggia VOR behind me, the Bologna VOR ahead, the ADF over Ferrara, the LORAN which can call up three stations over the Mediterranean and can calculate position and route on its own, the DME which measures distances from places and report points not visible to me, the transponder, the gyroscopes, the variometers, the altimeters—in other words, the house in my charge has a certain number of rooms. All this paraphernalia, which in a couple of years will be obsolete, could break down at any moment, but there would always be the floating compass, swaying and dragging, which every airplane, from the largest to the smallest, carries in its cockpit. The clock and compass were what I was trained to use years ago, long before being initiated into the ways of the electronic Ramayana; and Bruno, whom I had to thank for my apprenticeship, is here beside me, seated across from me. Bruno is in retirement now, not that anyone would dare pronounce that word in his presence. He does not mind accompanying me on longer journeys, shows greater affability now, the effect of the invisible wear of the years, but the relationship remains unchanged. With his spectacles rammed over his nose, like a cat in a fairy tale, he holds up in front of him the aeronautical chart with the first leg of the flight, towards Alghero. The chart is folded inside the pages of a book of photographs of Saint-Exupéry and Squadron II/33, taken in Alghero in the spring of '44. At intervals, Bruno raises his eyes from chart and photographs, peers out over his lenses with one of those looks which once caused me more concern than any situation in which I landed myself, then returns to the photographs. He is absorbed mainly by the P38 Lightning, the plane in which Saint-Exupéry disappeared. What an aircraft, he exclaims, two Mustang fighters joined at the wings! and he accompanies this notion with a tiny gesture of the hand. Everything in this flight proceeds normally.

0810 HOURS, HEADING 201°, 8500 FEET. CEILING AND
VISIBILITY OK.

Quite suddenly, the horizon opened out over the
Apennines, first the little circle of aerials whose signals
I had been following appeared in the woods on the
summit of Monte Croce, then the rest of the landscape
rose gradually to the surface like a meaning making
itself clear. Now Ginar and Marel are not simply vir-
tual landmarks but points that coincide with the curve
of a river, with the floor of a plain, with one of the
cities—Empoli? Pontedera? who could say?—which
grow more dense as they descend to the sea, a sea
already in sight, and with it the island of Elba. We
glide along Ambra 12, but the authentic contours of
the countryside itself, a rolling, chaotic incline of fields,
of water coursing towards the estuary, of jutting rock
which all make that landscape seem the verification of
a mental supposition, have been superimposed upon
the imaginary abstraction of the straight lines, little
triangles and radials which are the airway. At every
report point, I speak to the Air Traffic Control
Authority; there have been seven so far, courteous to
a man, and with each I have exchanged swift words,
honed down, as custom requires, to a professional
minimum. In the days of Saint-Exupéry, messages
were transmitted in Morse code, the radio operator
transcribed and passed to the pilot a sheet with a few
crucial words, and something of that concentration
lingered on in his books, in those brief, deeply intense,
somewhat peremptory phrases which circle around

facts as though the facts were a framework which there was neither the need nor the time to describe (and in any case, a fact in aviation lasts a very few seconds). The fact radiated an energy of feeling, fear, euphoria, sense of conflict, which preceded and followed it: the fact united freedom and responsibility. This link made a considerable impact on André Gide, who introduced *Vol de Nuit* to the French public with the words: Here a paradoxical truth is stated, that the fortune of man lies not in freedom but in the acceptance of a duty.

His characters and stories came from flight, but so too did the first inklings of a complex system of thought, elaborated over the years and not always totally coherent. The first strand was that notion of freedom as responsibility. It was that responsibility which weighed on his shoulders one evening in 1927 when Didier Daurat, the redoubtable director of the Latécoère company, announced to him that the following day he would be making his maiden postal flight from Toulouse to Casablanca. Responsibility was an anguished and inebriating experience, whose highest purpose was the transportation of the mail. With time it would become the freedom-cum-responsibility of those who chose the airline or desert "as others choose the monastery." Those others, apart from him, were Guillaumet and Mermoz, pilots in an age when meteorology was a diviner's art, when engines could cut out with no more warning than the sound of porcelain shattering and propellers spluttering, when radio bearings on ground beacons were nonexistent and when the only rule, unwritten but passed by word of mouth, was the briefing given to Saint-Exupéry by the field manager on the eve of his maiden flight with the air postal service: Navigating by compass in Spain is very fine, and most elegant, but just bear in mind that underneath those seas of cloud there is nothing but eternity.

We change altitude at the request of Control, who make us descend from eighty-five hundred to sixty-five hundred feet. I have the leisure to look over the populated areas along the Tuscan coast as far as the Punta di Piombino, and just beyond that I point Elba out to Bruno. From where do we "see" places when we name them; when we say Palermo, Sassari, Ancona, Ventimiglia or Buenos Aires, in what perspective do we utter these words? What is the image which speeds through the mind in the infinitesimal fraction of a second separating the city in the mind from the word which denotes it? If it were a city I knew, the image which emerged would be of a street or a house, or the emotion of a meeting, or regret over having failed to meet someone. Otherwise, I would imagine those cities in the region to which they belonged, within the political confines of a state, closed in a continent, I would name them from the point of view of a map. While flying, on the other hand, geography changes dimension, between the map which I keep folded on the laptop table and what I see outside there is scarcely any variation, geography is not the earth in writing but the earth itself lived in the passing.

A more deeply rooted feeling of responsibility—not

the mail but the nation—will make Saint-Exupéry
beg to return to the Air Force in the very Squadron
II/33 with which he had already fought the "phoney
war" in France, and which had based itself in Algiers
after the defeat. He was forty-three years old, too old
for the Lightning; training for that aircraft was like
starting from zero. Air reconnaissance was a complicated discipline, a mission could be entered as com-
pleted only if you came back with the photographs,
the real blow was struck against the enemy in the
darkroom, in the developing baths. He played his part
as far as they allowed him; he used to say, If I do not
play my part, how can I talk of my country? Everyone
gets what they want—he got his first sortie over the
south of France; on the second, returning to Algiers,
he overran the runway and slewed the plane into a
vineyard. The Americans took his plane away from
him.

0900 HOURS, HEADING 201°, 4500 FEET.

CEILING AND VISIBILITY OK.

Having passed the island of Montecristo on the left
some time ago, we are over open sea, under a scorch-
ing sun, one hundred and fifteen miles of sea with
only two report points, Bekos and Tallin, which only
electronic devices can pinpoint on the unchanging, ho-
mogeneous blue background broken only by a few
tiny boats with white foam in their wake. These are
still Italian territorial waters, but Bruno is already
bickering with the powerful French military radar at
Solenzara in Corsica which oversees the "prohibited

zone"—practically the whole of this area of the Tyrrhenian—we are overflying; he observes correct aeronautical procedure as he argues, so it is only possible to know that the two are engaged in an argument from the harshness of the voices, his and the air traffic controller's. That apart, each is happy to make his own case, and go no further; the zone is a firing range for jet fighters, either I climb to altitudes beyond the operational ceiling of our plane, or I enter a free, narrow air lane along the Corsican coast ("just in front of his house," as Bruno puts it, switching off the microphone), extending the flight considerably. The controller is repeating what I had already read on the AIP in the airport before taking off: "The zone is out of bounds every working day from sunrise to sunset;" Bruno replies, "All right," and I keep to the same course. If there are no problems, that is, if Solenzara does not call back, things generally proceed in this fashion: the operators say what they are required to say, we reply as we are required to reply, then I continue straight ahead, cutting across the sea as far as Olbia. Even flight has its Byzantine rituals.

An outstanding, instinctive, if undisciplined and absentminded, pilot—that was the judgment of his superiors, Daurat in the days of the Aéropostale, Alias at the time of the reconnaissance flight over Arras, Gavoille in the last days in Alghero and Bastia. At ten, first takeoff with a bicycle and sheet, takeoff aborted; at twenty, crashed at Le Bourget with a Hanriot HF14, which he had taken without authorization; at thirty-three, capsized in the Bay of Saint-Raphaël with a Latécoère seaplane which he was test-piloting, a profession for which he could not have been more unsuited; instead of coming down on the rear of the floats, he touched the water in horizontal flight nose slightly down, sinking the plane and almost drowning. On another Latécoère seaplane, the pilot's door, which he had neglected to secure, was wrenched off in midair. At thirty-five, on the Paris-Saigon run, for which he had prepared himself badly and at the last minute for the sake of the one-hundred-and-fifty-franc fee, he became convinced during the hours of darkness that he was over Cairo, pierced the bank of cloud to get sight of the sea, was still searching when his *Caudron Simoun* buried itself in the sand at two hundred and seventy kilometers an hour. He and his mechanic, Prévot, emerged from the plane unscathed but lost in the middle of the desert; they were picked up three days later by M. Emile Raccaud, manager of a remote branch of the Egyptian Salt & Soda Co. Ltd. At thirty-eight, during a New York–Tierra del Fuego flight, which served no purpose, not even financial, he landed in Guatemala, at a site which was not so much an airfield as a strip of grass furnished with a fuel pump. Somehow he managed to communicate with the pump attendant and get his fuel, but neglected to calculate how much was put in, that is, how much more the aircraft would weigh. He had to ask the attendant the best direction for takeoff, set off down the minuscule track, came to the end of it, got the *Caudron Simoun* airborne for a few seconds, only to see it belly-flop back to earth. Prévot emerged from the wreckage of the crash, which was one hundred percent unforgiving, with a broken leg, and Saint-

Exupéry with a fractured jaw, cuts all over his body, and a laceration of the collarbone which left him with ankylosis of the shoulder for the rest of his life. In later years, even if he had wished to eject from the Lightning, the old wound would have made it impossible, short of rolling the plane over, throwing open the canopy and dropping out.

For all that, he was an astonishing pilot, and these were things which, at that time, with those planes, on exploits like those, could easily happen. He was distrait and, after takeoff, became abstracted; some flights were long and tedious, he used to scribble notes in a logbook, and even on the morning of the last flight he had a little pad attached to his leg. "*Pourquoi risquons-nous si facilement notre vie pour acheminer des lettres?*" he asked the other pilots of Cap Juby, without expecting an answer, but anxious to know if they too were aware of the disproportion. Why risk our lives for a handful of letters? He was an excellent pilot, but not of the standard of Mermoz, or Guillaumet, his model, Guillaumet who had overflown the Andes three hundred and eighty-three times and on one occasion, after a crash, had survived five days on a glacier among the mountain peaks, Guillaumet who finally resolved to plod out of the mountains onto the plains so that his body would be discovered and his wife receive the insurance. When Guillaumet died many years later in the Mediterranean, Saint-Exupéry wrote: "I am Guillaumet's."

0945 HOURS, ALGHERO FERTILIA, RUNWAY 03-21.

WIND 160°, 6 KNOTS.

We were second in line to land, the DC9 which preceded us on final approach could be seen clearly on the opposite side of the circuit, then it was my turn. It is always an exhilarating moment, flight converting to glide, landing gear down, full flaps, the perspective gradually flattening out and reacquiring its normal appearance, then on the runway the pullback with the control column and the waiting, waiting until the ground reclaims you. I ought to speak of how we were welcomed at the airport's military base, of the courtesy of a group captain, of the charm of his office, of how he and his squadron leader stared in amazement at photos of that very airport fifty years previously, listening intently to a story they knew nothing of, but recognizing the hangar and the sheds which still stood around a runway which still ran in the same direction as then; of how the officer in his turn reconstructed the life of the base, left to run down after the war and reopened in the fifties, of how, as we walked among the hangars, Bruno pointed to some aging T6s, now covered in dust and left to rot, to the American twin-seater training machines on which, right here in Alghero, he had served his apprenticeship. I ought too to speak of the warm sun which filtered through the pinasters to light up the group captain's office with its trophies and souvenirs of old ceremonies, of the cicadas outside, and of Bruno and the others talking of forgotten airplanes, forgotten friends and common memories, and all the while asking question after question. They seemed like men of the sea, mariners meeting up in some port; and yet the airman is not the successor of the sailor, nor his modern equivalent, nor does the aircraft have the relationship to the sky that the ship has to the sea. Each ship has a character, soul and history of its own, but with aircraft the character adheres, if at all, to the model, mass produced by the thousand, and it is of the model alone that each pilot will gain familiarity and experience in a purely personal way. Further, relationships between people who fly are not forged in the air but on land, in discussions about flight, for on the aircraft there is not the human multiplicity of the crew, the passenger is alone with his neighbor, the crew will never number more than five or six, and however many there are, each one is too continually busy. An airplane is not like a ship, where the moral laws of the mainland are transferred to a more restricted, autonomous domain and tested to breaking point, an airplane retains nothing of land and home: in a ship people sleep, relax, plot, enjoy lengthy hours of idleness, endure stifling delays in ports; in an airplane there is no space for humdrum routine and the only valid rules are the operational rules of the air. Mistakes are committed, but these are almost invariably of a technical, and scarcely ever of a moral, nature. The human spirit needs time and space to uncover its inner darkness, to display its ignominy and depravity, and on a plane there is too little of both time and space; in other words, while airborne, human beings are temporarily deprived of their own evil, reduced to bewildered silence in the face of procedural routine. In flight, even those who make every effort to bring out the worst in themselves find themselves implacably condemned to a certain nobility of spirit.

This was the route which Saint-Exupéry took. What mattered to him more than the facts, which, as they occur, weave together an individual's destiny, were actions; the weight of intention is what distinguishes action from fact. His actions never had any savor of vitalism; indeed at conception they were often useless actions, whose necessity remained to be discovered or invented: the mission to Arras, the subject of *Flight to Arras*, was a wholly worthless enterprise in a France now on her knees, but was of value to him in allowing him to narrate a deep feeling of defeat, not merely the defeat of France but the defeat of the links which hold men together, an undoing of what unites man to Man, that is, to the best in himself, and of what permits the flow of the one to the other. In *Night Flight*, he had provided a genuine model of action, not in the pilot Fabien who runs the risks, goes missing and dies, but in Rivière, the airline chief, the man who does not take to the air, who remains behind his desk, who does not act himself but who determines the actions of others, experiencing even more torment over each and every act than if he were himself in the front line. The action was free of anything as trivial as adventure, courage was genuinely the last, the meanest, the most vainglorious of virtues. Above and beyond questions of airplanes, mail and war, his books constitute a meditation on the possibilities of humanism at the height of the twentieth century, a stand against collectivism as the mere arithmetical sum of individualities, a metaphysical examination of Being in solidarity with all the others. Action served only to establish bonding between men, it liberated love, it was like a mellow apperception which brought to light the nature of mere facts and underwrote their significance. The mystique of the bonding made of him an essentially religious writer, even if he had no truck with the names of God, preferring to halt on the threshold of his own questioning. None of it entirely devoid of grandiloquence, and with elements of the intense and the imprecise.

Once I was given the photograph of a sheet of paper on which, in the early days of '42 in America, he had listed, in lines of spidery writing scrawled over the page, the key concepts of *Citadelle*—the concept of the nomadic and the sedentary, concept of landscape constructed in passage, concept of the "marvellous collaboration," concept of questions which die, concept of the stones and silence, concept of Cook's travel agency, concept of the silence which nourishes and of slowness, concept of time which flows and time which fills, concept of the domain, concept of the bucket, the spade and the mountain, concept of the peace which is beatitude, death of replies and nonreconciliation.

1630 HOURS, IN SIGHT, 1000 FEET,
3/8 OF ALTOCUMULUS WITH BASE AT 5000 FEET.

Low flight, I hug as closely to the coastline of Corsica as if I were engaged in a tracing exercise, from which I only tear myself away to cut off over the little inlets after Bonifacio, the Gulf of Santa Manza and the Gulf of Porto Vecchio, and then I follow the coast itself. The route is this shoreline, so close at hand, scurrying in and out, dotted with chalets and boats.

With the autopilot off, I have less of the butler feeling, or rather, of the feeling of a butler afforded the freedom of staring out of the window and enjoying his ease. We had lingered too long with the officer in Alghero, and so I took Bruno to eat lobster and shellfish in the bay at Porto Conte. Put it down to the artificiality of flight, or to a need to compensate for nobility of spirit, but it is beyond doubt that there is an odd link between airplanes and food; in any case, with Bruno, it always ends like this. In reality, I brought him to Porto Conte for another meal, for a farewell lunch which took place fifty years ago—the lunch which Saint-Exupéry and John Phillips, the reporter and photographer from *Life* magazine, offered to Squadron II/33 the day before they left Alghero. They gathered in the villa where Gavoille and the other officers were billeted. The bay has remained as it was then, bleak and almost uninhabited. After the meal, I asked Bruno if he would like to help me find that villa; he cut a comic figure, sweating and engrossed, book in hand as he struggled among the brush. He peered at the two promontories which close off the gulf, compared them with the details of the photographs, said Higher up! a bit to the right! no, that's not it, taking the whole enterprise very seriously, as was his wont. The pictures of that party in the courtyard at nightfall give the impression of strange gentlemen, out of time, out of place, babbling in a mixture of languages; having exchanged light guns and machine guns for cameras, they were as poetical and unarmed as the Lightnings on which they flew.

Those who knew Saint-Exupéry in those days, or those who had known him even earlier in the Sahara, talk of the conjuring tricks he played, of his habit of playing the piano by rolling two oranges along the keyboard, of the chess matches or six-letter games which delighted him, and of the mathematical theorems he worked on hour after hour. He read few works of fiction, but devoured every kind of tract and curious work he requested of pilots returning from their travels. The outcome of such readings was invariably some experiment in physics or metaphysics, and some new number for his improvised performances. He was not given to pontificating, and appeared as curious as his listeners about the outcome of his own line of thought. He returned to Alghero after his sorties, approaching the landing strip with landing gear still up, leading everyone to wonder if there had been some mishap or oversight and to fire off warning rockets, call out ambulances and firefighting appliances; but halfway down the glide path he would flap the wings to signal it was all a joke, overshoot and come in again with the wheels in place.

Methodically, Bruno located the farewell lunch villa, partly modified, repainted at some unspecified time, then abandoned. I like museums, but I also like places seemingly without history, or more precisely, for which there was a history, but an unknown or forgotten one. My boyhood was filled with such houses, built with an eye for a space and design which defeat had ridiculed, abandoned after the war, silent houses with no tale to tell, where something had happened but no one could say exactly what. "Condemned" is the beautiful French expression for those walled-up doors and windows.

Ah yes, flying low along the coast, Bastia already in view, the tower operator a woman, who speaks the only kind of aeronautical English comprehensible in Corsica. I do a couple of rolls. I am happy. No, myths have nothing to do with it. Flight was inextricable from myth as long as it was not humanly feasible. After the invention of the aircraft, there remains only one thing in the world with which flight is really connected, and that is childhood. Pilots do not have feathered wings, they are not angels, much less heroes; they are child-adults, latent children, well looked after in their maturity, carefully preserved inside one of the professional guises life has assigned them, but tied to childhood by the elastic of the sling peeping out of their pockets. As to whether there is some special relationship between childhood and death, I wouldn't know.

1545 HOURS THE FOLLOWING DAY, BASTIA PORRETTA,
RUNWAY 16-34. WIND CALM.

We are at the holding point of runway sixteen, Bastia Porretta. I have omitted the weather report because it is a bit complicated. There are different types of cloud over the northwest Mediterranean, with their bases at different altitudes, but things are looking better now than a few hours ago. We await clearance for takeoff. Last night, we slept in Erbalunga, where the II/33 pilots were billeted in their Corsica days. I went with Bruno for a walk along the seafront; a pleasant, healthy breeze was blowing after the heat of the day. At dinner, in an old trattoria in the harbor area, he declared himself satisfied with the place and the wine, satisfied, and more than a little drunk, so much so that he allowed himself to talk about his wife and daughters, as well as about his plans for the future. At a certain point, he changed tone and glanced behind him: Do you think that this Saint-Exupéry, if he lived nearby, would have dropped in here to eat? I started laughing, said I've no idea, perhaps he did, could be, maybe he sat in that very seat facing the fishing boats, maybe he smoked or stared at the night, who knows what was in his mind?

Now, at the holding point of runway sixteen, Bruno looks over at the control tower as though expecting clearance to arrive with a wave of the hand rather than over the radio. This morning I took him along to the old airport at Borgo, a dozen or so kilometers further up the road. Behind the barracks of the Armée de Terre, we came across the old grass airstrip which ran from the lagoon to the hill. A grass airstrip is in no way different from a grass field, and yet it can be clearly seen that this was once a runway. In the thin sunlight and the fresher air, we walked its full length, from one end almost to the other. It was still possible to make out, in the undergrowth, the beaten earth taxiways. On one side, there was a little metal ruin, a rusted, open turret, with traces of the original white and red still visible.

"India Golf India Oscar Mike, cleared for lineup and takeoff, one six. Then turn left."

After takeoff, we proceed in a wide, leftward curve, gaining enough height over the sea to allow us to overfly the hill. Then we turn the nose northwest. At one in the afternoon of the thirty-first of July, 1944, Gavoille had already put out calls to all Allied radar stations in the northern Mediterranean. No one had seen them. Those who were with Gavoille in the operations room were to recall the frantic tones with which he demanded information, the increasingly implausible hypotheses he put forward to explain the late arrival, until time marked the limits of the Lightning's self-sufficiency. Of waiting of this kind, when it had been the turn of Mermoz over the Atlantic, Saint-Exupéry had said: "I know nothing more tragic than these delays. A companion does not land at the expected time. There is silence from another who was due to arrive, or send a signal. And when ten minutes have passed, a period of waiting which in our day-to-day lives would scarcely even be noticed, suddenly everything grows tense. Fate has made its entry. It holds men in its thrall. Sentence has been delivered on them. Fate has made its judgment, and we can only hold our breath." Towards evening, someone, after attaching a passport photo of Saint-Exupéry to the page, wrote in the squadron logbook, *"Non rentrée."*

What Gavoille failed to discover that afternoon, he failed to discover for the rest of his days, and it was to remain a mystery to everyone else. Of all the possible or probable accounts, I preferred Gavoille's own, which with time became an obsession; he never abandoned the quest. In the early stages, he believed there had been a failure of the oxygen supply. When they reached a certain altitude, the pilots opened the cylinders and took their first breath of paint-scented air from Massachusetts or Ohio. Saint-Exupéry, big and bulky as he was, consumed more oxygen than the others, he might have had some problem, he had once before forgotten to switch on the oxygen supply, he might have lost consciousness and fallen forward against the control column, causing the plane, with its engines on full throttle, to go into a dive, to disintegrate as it plunged at speed through the air, and to end up in the sea. Then, towards the end of the seventies, Gavoille, by now General René Gavoille (retired), who had never ceased asking at the foot of his articles on Saint-Exupéry if anyone had seen or heard anything, received from the Côte d'Azur recollections and eyewitness accounts. The Côte d'Azur must have been beautiful that day in '44, even more beautiful than it is now to Bruno and me as, after a hundred miles of open sea, we catch our first glimpse of it under a sky of high cloud fleeing eastward. Each morning the war had something to offer, and that morning too there was the spectacle of a Lightning flying very low from the mountains, from the valley to the north of Biot, flying low and fast, pursued by two German fighters: a stream of white smoke was coming out of the starboard engine of the Lightning, then the plane went over on one side, did a somersault over the water and disappeared. Several people described the same scene to Gavoille, each in full agreement over place and time—shortly after midday. Others simply remembered having seen a plane of the Lightning type crash into the sea, and Saint-Exupéry's was the only one to have disappeared that morning in the northwest Mediterranean. The following day, the trainee-pilot Robert Heichele, who was twenty years old and who was to die in action two weeks later, wrote to a friend of his that he had shot down a Lightning on the thirty-first of July, 1944. He and Sergeant Hogel, on board their "Big Nose" FW 190, had intercepted it between Logis and Castellane, along Napoleon's highway. "It was flying some two thousand feet above us," said Heichele in his report, "so we were unable to attack it; to our astonishment, it turned and started a descent, it seemed to be coming towards us. I did a climbing spiral and took up firing position one hundred and fifty feet from its tail. I fired but missed. I executed a barrel roll, regaining a good position, fired once more but the shots passed in front of the plane. He attempted to shake me off by going into a nosedive; I pursued him and when I was thirty meters from him, unleashed another volley. I saw a trail of white smoke emerge from his starboard engine; the plane flew low along the coast, then plunged into the sea."

It may be that I prefer this version because it is the least mysterious, less in keeping with any hypothesis of suicide, pilot error or accident, or perhaps because it is the most aeronautical, or perhaps because more than any other it lends itself to falsification, if it could be shown that Heichele had never existed and that his letter was a forgery. Be that as it may, the sea is the same sea here underneath us, so close it could be touched, the sea off Saint-Tropez, Saint-Raphaël, Antibes, the sea whose surface I am skimming at top speed. Bruno taps his index finger on the altimeter beside him, and when I fail to take notice taps the altimeter on my side, When you fly like this, you've got to be careful, there's an optical illusion that makes you think you are higher than you are, better take your eyes off the water and fix them on the instrument panel. Bruno does no more than tap his finger on the instruments, because he is sure he taught me all this years ago. Bruno is still Bruno.

On the phone, René Gavoille had a calm, alert voice. I spoke to him before setting off, he said: "That morning, he was not supposed to be flying, it was pure chance, I stayed in my bed because we had been up late the night before, he got up early, he hardly ever slept at night, he went to the officer in charge and obtained permission for takeoff. He shouldn't have been flying, my orders were precise, but such is destiny. It was the only time I wasn't there, a sortie he was not supposed to be on, a useless mission, considering the dangers involved and the imminent landing in Provence. He went over Savoy and took his photos. On his way back, when he had already been hit, he gave in to another of his surges of emotion and passed one more time over the places of his boyhood and adolescence. He lies there, in that sea. You can imagine what happens when an airplane doing four hundred kilometers an hour crashes into the water."

I pull at the control column, I have gained sufficient height, I dip my wings twice or three times in salute. Bruno is calmer now. Nice and Menton appear on the left. We do not speak, but then we hardly ever speak in flight. Each of us is already thinking of Genoa and

Milan, of Venice and of the almost straight line which will take us to Venice and home. At nightfall, after landing, we will take long, elastic strides to shake off the fatigue of the controls. We will smile, reunited once again with our shadows.

DELGIUDI Del Giudice,
        Daniele.

        Takeoff.

003649   9473120

BAKER & TAYLOR